For Your Maker is You

For Your
Maker
is Your
Husband

A Study of the
Christian Understanding of Selfhood

PAULINE WARNER

EPWORTH PRESS

First published 1991
by Epworth Press
1 Central Buildings, Westminster, London SW1H 9NR

Typeset by J&L Composition Ltd, Filey, North Yorkshire
and printed in Great Britain by
Clays Ltd, St Ives plc

CONTENTS

All that I am I give to you
All that I have I share with you
Within the love of God, Father, Son and Holy Spirit

(Marriage Service of Church of England:
The Alternative Service Book 1980)

1

Introduction:

Divine and Human Selfhood

One of the prevalent concerns of modern thought is to develop an adequate expression of human selfhood or personhood: an expression which does justice to the complexity, distinctiveness and freedom of each individual human being while simultaneously affirming the interdependence of human beings with each other, and indeed with inanimate objects such as the environment in which they live or the temporal events with which they are involved.

The problem of arriving at such an adequate expression lies in the fact that any definition must take into account several paradoxes and tensions in human nature. Such a definition must include the individuality and uniqueness of each person, that fundamental 'I'ness which is experienced by the self-aware person who knows that he[1] is distinct and separate from all other 'I's and the inanimate world. This distinctiveness points to the freedom of each individual to act as he chooses and to be responsible for his own life. It is clearly manifest in what is known as 'the personality' of that individual: the particular set of responses and behaviour which becomes characteristic of that individual so that other people may be able to identify him as a recognizable unity. That person, though complex and changing, is nevertheless experienced as a consistent continuum which comes to be recognized as that distinctive human being. Of course, that does not mean that any human being can ever be fully understood either by herself or others because there is an essential mystery about each person which also must be taken into account in any attempt at definition.

That mystery is at least partly explained by the evolutionary nature of human personality, the fact that a person's character is not static from birth but develops and changes under the influence of new circumstances and experiences. Indeed, this fact is such an important factor in any definition of 'being' that some philosophers have even suggested that the word 'being' itself is misleading because it implies an unchanging static entity and have suggested that human beings are best described in terms of 'becoming'. As far as this study is concerned, this idea is most explicitly represented by the philosophers and theologians of the Process school but it is an understanding which is assumed by many of the other writers and thinkers whose work is included.

The fact that a person is growing and changing in response to her circumstances points to another complex tension in human nature. For on the one hand, her response to a particular event or person involves her own freedom and capacity to make a specific decision and act in a particular way. As there is no guarantee how she will respond such an experience is one of the clearest signs of the free-will and independence of any one human being. But, on the other hand, such an experience also points to the essential relatedness and interdependence of persons, and indeed inanimate objects: for the same personality which reacted freely and independently has been shaped and moulded by the influence of other people, the environment in which she has lived and the experiences which she has gone through previously. In addition, any response she makes will further mould her own personality and may well influence other people and affect the environment and future events. Thus any idea of human freedom being displayed in one absolutely detached, independent being standing foursquare against the world and other people is shown to be fallacious. Indeed, the fundamental contention of this study is that true personhood is found only by being 'in relationship' with others. To be more accurate, relationship is an ontologically-given characteristic of human beings who are part of a complex matrix of mutuality and interdependence which is dynamic and expansive. True personhood is realized when that ontological given is recognized and accepted. Yet that ontological characteristic of relationship does not preclude the insistence that each individual is free to choose not to enter into relationship or alternatively free to choose to share himself with others.

Human beings are also part of a continuum with the rest of reality, both temporal and spatial, which although it is inanimate can appropriately be spoken of as 'affecting' and 'being affected by' human persons. In recent years, there has been an increasing interest in the belief that the whole of reality is interconnected. Such interest has been manifest in ecological concern and even in animistic beliefs. These popular movements have drawn inspiration from the revolution in scientific and philosophical thought, moving away from the Newtonian world-view to one associated with the name of Einstein. The further insights of quantum physics are obviously more complex and sophisticated than a simple assertion that all things are connected together but it is nevertheless true that any world view of the twentieth century must take into account the belief that all reality is organically related and not a collection of disparate entities. So any adequate concept of personhood must assume that relationship is a fundamental characteristic of all human beings. That assumption, however, must be balanced with the affirmation of the particularity, distinctiveness and freedom of any one human being.

In describing that one human being in post-Enlightenment culture, such a description should include an appreciation of the intellectual capacity of the human mind for rational thought and expression, for it is that particular capacity which, for the most part, marks the uniqueness of human-kind. It is also the development of that capacity which explains the liberating of humanity from primitive superstition and enables humans (to a certain extent) to understand and control their environment and temporal events. However, the term 'rationality' must not be too narrowly defined and it is increasingly being argued that modern Western culture has over-emphasized the rational, logical capacities of human beings to the detriment of other parts of the human personality such as emotional responses, moral stances or the power of the imagination and creative ability. It has become somewhat fashionable to speak of the rational and non-rational components of the human psyche, for example in the theory that the brain is composed of two distinct hemispheres, the right side controlling the intuitive and imaginative and the left hand side the logical and rational. Any adequate conception of 'the person' must accommodate this particular tension, but a simple juxtaposition of these two separate capacities does not do justice to the complexity of human nature, and there will always be a danger that one side is over-emphasized to the downgrading of the other. Far more satisfactory as an expression of the human mind is a conception which recognizes that both components are integrated with each other, and that the term 'rationality' includes both sides. An adequate definition of selfhood must express that complex understanding of rationality.

The next tension in human nature is, ironically, somewhat difficult to express in terms of opposites. This is the tension between the physical and the non-physical. The problem arises in trying to find a suitable word to express the opposite of physical because neither 'mental' nor 'spiritual' is satisfactory. However, as far as this introduction is concerned, it is sufficient to state that the physical body is an integral part of selfhood, that a person 'does not have a body, but is a body'.

Words such as 'personality' may suggest an amorphous essence which is somehow located within a body, but the assumption of this study will be that such dualism is false, and the body is an integral part of the human person. There can be thus no simplistic distinction between 'body' and 'soul'. A person experiences through her body and she communicates her personality through her physical acts (both consciously and unconsciously). Therefore, any definition of 'the person' must assume this wholeness of physical and non-physical.

Yet another paradox or tension is that between the capacity for good and evil in humanity. On the one hand, humanity has the potential for immense good and displays that in love, compassion, self-sacrifice, wisdom and artistic, rational and cultural achievement. On the other hand, it is capable also of destructiveness, folly, irrational behaviour, selfishness and cruelty. Often this tension is experienced in the same way as by St Paul: 'I can will what is right but I cannot do it. For I do not do the good I want, but the evil I do not want is what I do' (Rom. 7.18–19). It can also be seen in terms of intentional evil and even on such a scale that it provokes the adjective 'inhuman'. It has become almost trite to say that in the twentieth century, following the Holocaust and Hiroshima, the question of explaining this paradox is especially pressing, but the fact that it is said so often indicates its importance. Any expression of human personhood must at least recognize this tension even if it does not attempt to explain it.

Such a brief summary can hardly include all the components of human nature, but the very number of qualifications used in the foregoing description has served to show the problem of drawing up any definition of human personhood. The final tension to be mentioned points to the specifically theological aim of this work: the tension between a person's sense that he is a self-determining being able to direct his own life and the sense that ultimately he must accept the givenness of his life and must learn to surrender himself to that givenness. This particular tension is acknowledged by most philosophical systems, but responses to it vary. It is possible, for example, to accept this tension in purely humanistic terms, but it is in this tension perhaps more than any other that the religious perspective can be introduced. In that case, it is appropriate to speak of the human 'sense of createdness', although it must be emphasized that these words do not define the nature of the one who creates, but are simply used to express one part of human experience.

It is not the aim of this study to be a philosophical examination of, or justification for, religious belief. Neither is its intention to compare different religions or systems of thought. Its aim is to be a conceptual exploration of the statement of traditional Christian teaching that true personhood is realized in relationship with God who has revealed himself in Jesus Christ and is experienced through the Holy Spirit, an exploration which will be made in terms of the key metaphor of marriage. This statement will be examined and argued to be consistent with modern philosophical beliefs and not, as is popularly held, contradictory to modern thought. There will be no full discussion of comparative religion, but it is perhaps important to emphasize at the beginning what will turn out to be one of the cardinal themes of this work: that although Christian belief should always be prepared to receive truth from other religions and philosophies it is that very scandal of particularity which lies at the heart of the Christian faith which not only makes it distinctive among religious systems but which makes it conceptually satisfactory. I do not condone an unthinking dismissal of non-Christian beliefs, but do assert the scandal of particularity of God's involvement with one specific people, the church, and his supreme revelation in one man, Jesus Christ, as not only fundamental Christian dogma but appropriate to the categories and concepts of human experience. As such, this work intends to argue that an adequate expression of human selfhood, taking into account the tensions which have been mentioned, is found in the Christian faith.

Critique of classical theism

That such an adequate expression of the human person is encouraged by Christian belief is a statement which needs justification, for in a great deal of contemporary society belief in God is held to be degrading to humanity rather than enhancing. As Jürgen Moltmann has suggested, any relationship between God and mankind has been seen as a struggle between rivals. 'In their struggle against each other theism and atheism begin from the pre-supposition that God and man are fundamentally one being. Therefore what is ascribed to God must be taken from one man and what is ascribed to man must have been taken from God.'[2] The problem of arriving at a satisfactory definition of human selfhood is increased in theological thought, which must seek to develop an adequate understanding of the selfhood of both God and human beings, and also conceive language for talking about the relationship between them.

Indeed, it is that belief in a relationship between God and humanity which has become so difficult to believe, as the quotation from Moltmann indicates. However, as that quotation also implies, such a problem arises in theism, the classical philosophical conception of God which has dominated Western religious thought since Aquinas. It is now frequently argued that this particular theistic conception is not adequately Christian, and many modern theologians, including Moltmann, are developing new understandings of divine activity and involvement in the world, believing with him that 'without a revolution in the concept of God there is no revolutionary theology'.[3] Indeed such is the philosophical and theological impasse caused by this conception that it has almost become a theological commonplace to state that the phrase 'God is dead' is not the slogan of downright atheism but an indication of the demise of that particular philosophical conception.

The concept of God as shaped by classical theism was 'a picture of the one changeless, infinite, perfect abstract absolute'. This picture reinforces the idea of such a gulf between God and mankind that it is difficult to envisage any kind of relationship between them. This particular criticism will be examined in detail later. Here, it is suggested, somewhat ironically, it was this specific model of God which has developed logically into the possibility of atheism. For in the

Five Ways by which Aquinas sought to answer the question
whether God exists there was already a tendency towards
Deism in the fact that the transcendence of God was emphasized to a degree that he was detached from any involvement
in creation. That tendency was advanced by Newtonian
physics, which showed that the solar system was a closed,
self-regulating entity which operated according to fixed
natural laws. As such, there was no need for any involvement by God. Belief in God, therefore, tended towards belief
in a Deistic Creator who initially set the universe 'in motion'
but was thereafter uninvolved. The advance of Kantian and
Humean philosophy reinforced that tendency by arguing
that the finite world did not necessarily provide an analogy
to infinity. Whereas for Aquinas the material world itself
mirrored the immaterial, Hume and Kant argued that this
procedure was invalid because there was no inherent
rationality, no logos, in the nature of the created world which
sanctioned the conclusions that classical theism had drawn.
In terms of relationship, the cardinal feature of classical
theism was the distinction between God and mankind, a
distinction which seemed to make any kind of continuous
relationship impossible and God's activity in the world was
limited to the occasional intervention. Further, because in the
neo-Platonic philosophy which undergirded Thomist theology, ideal form was considered more important than imperfect matter, interest tended to concentrate on the Supernatural Deity. The advance of phenomenalist philosophy
and natural science has meant that interest has concentrated
on the natural world as interesting and important in its own
right and not simply as a mirror of eternity. The separateness
has been maintained but the focus of attention has shifted
from one partner to the other.

Following the ideas of Kant and Newton, in the nineteenth
century Darwin promulgated the theory of evolution. This
apparently further challenged the Christian doctrine of
creation and was seen in some quarters as proof of the
falsity of Christian claims. However, others continued to
reconcile the claims of scientific theory with Christian belief.

Theologically the idea of evolution suggested an alternative model to Deism because God could be conceived as bound up with the actual processes of creation, creating continually instead of once at the beginning of time. So in idealist philosophy and particularly in the work of Hegel an essentially immanentist understanding of God was developed which was very different from the supernaturalism of the classical deity.

The advance of Einsteinian physics has done much to modify the rigid determinism of the Newtonian system as well as the absolutes of both Newton and Kant. However, it has not done this by reverting to anything like the classical picture, particularly in the recognition that time plays such an important part in the modern philosophical world-view. Einstein relativized the Newtonian absolutes of space and time by showing that all frameworks of reference are related and that there is a complex relationship between space, time, energy and matter. The implications of this for Christian theology are still being worked out, but one result has been to acknowledge the sheer contingency of the universe. This further challenges the Thomist concept which asserted the foreknowledge of God and it certainly denies the possibility of predestination. Indeed, it also challenges the Newtonian concept of creation as a closed order of cause and effect. There can be no absolute certainty as to what will happen in the future and so it becomes impossible to speak of the foreknowledge of God.

Scientific and philosophical concepts have all challenged the classical model of God and from that challenge it is a logical possibility to deny the existence of God in the atheism which characterizes modern thought. However, it is also possible to maintain a reasonable belief in God, but this belief must be able to accommodate these concepts in order to affirm the intellectual capacity of human persons. Language about God will only be understandable and effective today if it meets the criteria of truth and meaning generally established within the human community.

Within this general survey of intellectual developments

there are two specific concepts which need to be highlighted: the impassibility of God and divine power. It is the question of the impassibility of God which, perhaps more than any other, has shed doubts on the classical ideal of God. In that traditional ideal, God was held to be unchanging and immutable, acting upon the world and yet not acted upon by it. This idea has particularly raised problems in the modern world-view in which change has been recognized as so fundamental to identity. Put simply, the question is that in seeking to understand human persons it has been recognized that a person's being lies in his becoming. If God is then to be conceived of as in any way personal, how can it be that he never changes at all?

That question can then be taken a stage further and applied to the subject of relationship between God and mankind. Aquinas denied the possibility of any relationship in God himself because he denied the possibility of change.

> It is clear that being related to God is a reality in creatures, but being related to creatures is not a reality in God.
>
> When we speak of His relation to creatures we can apply words implying temporal sequence and change in the creatures just as we can say that the pillar has changed from being on my left to being on my right, not through any alteration in the pillar but simply because I have turned round.[4]

John Macquarrie has termed monarchical[5] an understanding of God in which God's transcendence over the world has been seen as so complete that there is no real relationship between them. The world is recognized to need God but God does not need the world. Similarly God affects the world but is not affected by it.

Modern understanding of relationships has shown that in any relationship the two partners are changed by each other. Again, the question needs to be asked that if God is to be understood as in any way personal he must surely be open to change by his relationship with humanity. Some theologians, perhaps most notably the feminist theologians, argue that it is precisely this hierarchical, asymmetrical 'relationship' between God and mankind which has sanctioned the hierarchies of human society in which one partner dominates the other. In order to create a more equitable, loving society they suggest that a new model of the divine–human relationship needs to be developed, a model which emphasizes the mutuality, intimacy and vulnerability of each partner in a true relationship of love. For, as the final point of this brief critique of classical theism, it needs to be recognized that such a God cannot be vulnerable. Yet again modern attention to the understanding of relationship has emphasized that both partners are vulnerable towards each other and in that vulnerability they experience pain. The classical God, however, cannot experience that pain nor, apparently, can he share the pain of his beloved as a human partner can. In the face of the world's suffering such an apathetic God can hardly be described as loving, for his impassibility means that he cannot experience genuine compassion. In the wake of atrocities of the twentieth century, the traditional question of theodicy, 'How can God be both utterly powerful and utterly loving?', becomes imperative. The traditional theistic model of God affirmed his absolute powerfulness but, apparently, at the cost of his loving. As Schubert Ogden has written:

> The deep reason for a theological rejection of classical metaphysics is not that such an outlook no longer commends itself to reasonable men, important as it is that we should recognize that fact and face up to its implications. No, the more profound reason is that such a metaphysics never has allowed, and in principle, never could allow, an appropriate theological explication of the central theme of Wesley's evangelical witness that God is love.[6]

The classical model, then, affirms the divinity of God in its understanding of his power but denies his personhood in terms of his capacity for loving relationship. It also denies the authentic selfhood of humans both intellectually and in the sense that a relationship with such an apathetic, impassible Being apparently degrades human beings rather than enhances them.

Any alternative model to this must preserve the power of God as well as affirming the relationship of God with humans and the integrity and capacity of human beings. In order to merit the name of 'Love', God must be shown to share in the sufferings and pains of the creatures whom he loves and yet in order to merit the ascription of divine power he must not be overwhelmed by such suffering but be able to rise above it.

The paradoxes of human selfhood have now been mirrored by the paradoxes of divine selfhood. The theological task, therefore, remains one in which those two distinctive selfhoods with all their complexity are brought together in a relationship which preserves both divinity and humanity and yet does not set them in opposition to each other. Walter Kasper has described this task of theology as concern with

> the mystery of an unfathomable love, the very essence of which is to unite what is distinct while respecting the distinction; for love is, in an almost paradoxical way, the unity of two who, while remaining distinct and essentially free, nevertheless cannot exist the one without the other.[7]

God as Lover or God as husband?

The same understanding of the theological task has inspired Norman Pittenger to suggest that a new model of God needs to be developed which images God as the cosmic Lover:

> It is appropriate and helpful to speak of God as the cosmic Lover ... because such a picture stresses the personal relationship which in religious life is enjoyed between that loving activity we call God, that basic thrust and drive in the cosmos whose quality is Love, and those who open themselves to it.[8]

It was this paragraph in particular, and the work of Pittenger and other Process theologians in general, which provided the initial intuition for this study. The idea of a relationship between two lovers implies mutuality, vulnerability and commitment as well as the suggestion that the two partners are enhanced by each other. As such, the model of God as Lover holds great potential as a complementary or even alternative model to the traditional pictures of God such as God as Father or God as King.

Since Christianity has already made use of the lanuage of human love in the mystical tradition and the nuptial imagery of the Bible there is apparently scope for developing such a modern thought with traditional imagery.

Such was my original intention but, working in accordance with the same process of understanding which will be examined later, that original 'hunch' or intuition was subjected to disciplined, rational thought and in that process the concepts underlying Process thought were found to be inadequate. For, although Pittenger completes the paragraph quoted above with the acknowledgment that 'when we speak strongly of love we understand that we are not using a word which suggests weakness, sentimentality or undemanding toleration of anything and everything', I argue later that the God which Process theology images does apparently tolerate anything and everything, or to be more accurate, he lacks the ability to act in such a way as to make any discrimination effective. The weakness of Process theology is its understanding of the will and freedom of God, but neither is its understanding of human personhood satisfactory. The overarching world-view of Process theology, especially in its reconciliation of evolutionary theory and Christian doctrine, seems conceptually satisfactory but on closer study it becomes questionable whether any system which fails to do justice to specific people and particular events is adequate. Similarly, the picture which it proposes of the relationship between God and humanity seems attractive, but the very emphasis on mutuality and intimacy which makes it so attractive is in danger of denying the

distinctiveness of each partner. The overall deficiency of the
Process system is that it cannot accommodate specificity and
particularity.

In a sense, that deficiency is already implied in the image
of God as Lover, for a lover does not necessarily have to
make a commitment to one particular relationship, whereas
such a commitment is demanded in marriage. Given that
fact, it is of great significance that when, in traditional
Christianity, human love has been used as an analogy for the
relationship between God and humanity, it has usually been
in terms of seeing God as Husband.

That which Process theology apparently cannot accommodate is what orthodox Christianity has always asserted: that
God freely chose to reveal his nature, which is Love, through
one specific man and that, in order to communicate his love,
which is available to all, he entered into a covenant with one
specific people.

The characteristics of love

The use of the analogy with a human love relationship allows
the possibility of speaking of God in terms of characteristics of love, some of which have already been noted
as incompatible with the classical theistic conception: vulnerability, intimacy and mutuality. These need to be expanded in order to provide an adequate phenomenology of
love.

By its most simple definition love implies a relationship
with another, a being-for and living-for a Thou who is
external to oneself. More precisely, it can be defined as a
dialectical-dialogical mode of being; dialectical because of
the almost paradoxical way in which the loving I feels that
it is only in that relationship with the beloved Thou that
she is really her true self. In love the I no longer wants
to be that I without this Thou. More than that, love involves
a redefinition of that loving I whose previous self-identity is
disturbed and even lost until it is discovered anew in the
response of the beloved. 'In the event of love the being of
lovers can be both gained and lost, both forfeited and

preserved – preserved by the beloved Thou and not by the loving I.'[9]

The dialectic is still more complicated in that the loving I does not simply want the Thou nor is content with her new selfhood until the beloved turns to her and wants to have her in the same way, as a Thou in whom he discovers his real self. It is imperative for a loving relationship that both partners see one another as a Thou, or, perhaps even better defined, that they see each other as an I. By this I mean to distinguish between true love and an irresponsible using of another person as if he were an It. Love includes respect for, and responsibility towards the other, recognizing his distinctiveness as a person and that he is not simply an object to be manipulated. This is not true love because ultimately it is a selfish seeking for self-gratification: the I has already decided what he is going to 'get out of' the other whether it be sexual gratification, an egotistic boost, material advantage or the status of being married.

In real love, there is no such pre-judged manipulation or decision: the lover is completely selfless in the sense that he does not demand any particular thing (or indeed anything) except to be possessed by the beloved, although in such a way that he is also viewed as a Thou not to be manipulated or abused. Real love is utterly selfless in that it demands nothing for itself, but in that selflessness (which is purely spontaneous) receives so much. This dialectic of love is almost impossible to express but the definition given by Eberhard Jungel may assist in our conceptualization: 'love is that great self-relatedness which is even more a still greater selflessness'. In other words, a person is most truly herself when she gives herself away in love and focusses not on herself but on her beloved.

Love is also dialogical. By this I mean two things. Firstly, it is a manifestation of sharing in love that a couple want to communicate their love with each other. The strength of love is such that they feel compelled to give expression to it, and although such expression is not always verbal (gestures, actions and simply being with the beloved are, of course, some of the most eloquent communications), the verbal communication is an important, and indeed necessary part of that sharing. That it is necessary is due to the fact that the two partners, although united in the union of love, are still distinct beings and therefore need a communication which will overcome the division, one which gives clear expression and confirmation of their love.

Secondly, love is dialogical in the sense that, in love, both partners continually address one another and respond to each other. By this I do not mean the explicit verbalization such as 'I love you' which was referred to in the previous paragraph, but the continuing process of being-in partnership in which each person becomes their self through the lover's influence and attention and in response to the selfhood of the other. Human being is not a static pre-social substance but a response to an external address. Once again, this is both an indication of, and made necessary by, the distinctiveness of each partner. The evolving selfhood of each partner could be said to be 'called forth' by the address of the other. The lover delights to see his beloved develop into her full selfhood, he recognizes latent possibilities in her which might need to be 'called forth' and his addressing of her will, therefore, be encouraging and attentive to her. However, such is love's stance of respect for, and responsibility towards, the distinctiveness of the beloved that he will not coerce nor manipulate her in any way. This is the risk of love: the response to his address may be rejection or denial, and the social nature of human being means that the beloved is also a being-in-relationship with, and addressed by others who will also 'call forth' that person's becoming in a way that the lover can never control. However, if the love is reciprocated then the dialectic of being, the self-relatedness which is selflessness, is both expressed in dialogue and is itself continuously dialogical.

All these concepts give rise to one word which summarizes the definition of love: love is pure overflow, overflowing being for the sake of another and only then for the sake of itself. All the ideas of love which have been noted are expressed by this word 'overflow' and since it suggests not only a 'flowing between' two persons but a 'flowing out' of one particular being, it preserves both the particularity and unity of lovers. This word also communicates the expanding of self which is effected in love, whereby barriers between persons (and maybe also between persons and the inanimate world) are broken down because they become inadequate. Language of expansionism and overflow itself leads to another comment on the definition of love: in order to define love more than superlatives are required. Love is more than perfect, more than fair, more than full, more than necessary, etc. The stretching of human language and concepts is hereby illustrated as effectively as any other way.

These ideas, concepts and images drawn from the observation of human love do not necessarily refer exclusively to sexual love between man and woman. They are just as descriptive of the love between, for example, parent and child or between friends. This is obvious because the nature of love cannot vary in kind between different loving relationships. While acknowledging this fact I nevertheless intend to focus on married love as an especially appropriate analogy of God's love with humanity. Again, it perhaps needs to be clarified that such concentration does not intend to imply that married love is necessarily better than love between unmarried lovers. Realistic observation of human relationships would quickly dispel such a myth. However, for the purpose of this work, the ideal of married love makes explicit certain ideas which are especially appropriate and which are not necessarily explicit in unmarried sexual love.

1. Firstly, the self-giving of marriage partners is complete in that it includes the physical and material as well as the emotional.

2. The temporal element of marriage ('until death us do part') will be argued to be significant in the discussion of the will and intention as well as the self's becoming which involves the future.

3. The particularity of commitment made to a specific

partner is extremely important. This is partly because it is within the limitations circumscribed by such a commitment that love is realistically worked out. It is also an affirmation that it is that specific Thou which awakens love in the loving self. The lover loves one particular person as her beloved and in doing so 'selects' that person and no other but such selection is not made on the basis of comparison with others. It is purely gratuitous, unpredictable and awakened by the sight of that one specific person. Particular commitment thus not only affirms the freedom and choice of the loving self but simultaneously (and without contradiction) affirms the compulsion which she experiences which might be expressed as 'she has no choice but to love that one'. This paradox will throughout be referred to as 'the necessity of love'.

It is because 'Husband' carries connotations of a freely-willed, complete commitment that I will argue that it is a more accurate and appropriate picture than 'Lover' to use when speaking of God.

The revelation of God

That God chooses to involve himself with one people is correlative to the belief that he is known through revelation and not by reason. Both classical theism and Process theology attempt to explain knowledge of God in terms of human philosophical categories, whereas orthodox Christianity has always maintained that God cannot be contained by these categories but reveals himself to whom he wills. Knowledge of God is not, therefore, an achievement of human consciousness but a gift bestowed through God's free grace. In maintaining that conviction the church has thereby maintained the prevenience of God's action and the priority of God over created reality.

Indeed, such a conviction is an alternative response to the decline of classical theism; since revealed truths do not depend upon philosophical categories for their proof, the questionings outlined earlier in this chapter do not undermine them as they do the tenets of traditional theism. This response is particularly associated with the name of Karl Barth. For him and other theologians some of whom, such as Torrance, Moltmann and Jüngel, will be included in this work, the starting point for theology is what God has revealed about himself. They would argue that any doctrine of God entails thinking through consistently and radically what Jesus Christ has revealed about God and that the most fundamental criticism of both classical and neo-classical theism is that it is simply not Christian enough. As John Macquarrie expresses it:

> Where we go wrong is that we bring along some ready made idea of God, wherever we may have learned it, and then try to make Jesus Christ fit in with that idea. If we take the idea of a revelation of God in Christ seriously then we must be willing to have our understanding of God corrected and even revolutionized by what we learn in Jesus Christ.[10]

Our conceptualization of love, in which the self finds its true self by turning to, and living in, the Other should make it reasonably easy to appreciate how human beings can be fulfilled by turning towards God as he reveals himself to be and not as human minds have pre-judged him. Yet although, as has already been suggested, revelation does not need the support of any theological justification. I will argue in the third chapter that it is not philosophically anachronistic and indeed can be argued to be more appropriate to modern thought than the concepts employed by the neo-classical theism of Process theology. So recognizing that the intellect can be fully engaged in a relationship with God who reveals himself as he wills is not problematical.

The problem in speaking of God in terms of the marriage analogy arises because of the danger of falling into the impasse which was outlined in the opening discussion: if the emphasis is placed on the equality between partners, then God loses his transcendence and therefore, by definition, his divinity. If, on the other hand, his superiority is maintained then the integrity of human beings is denied for they cannot be free, responsible partners in this relationship. It is at this point that the conceptualization of love outlined above must be rigorously applied, and I suggest that this impasse can be overcome by 'working through consistently and radically' what it means to say that God is Love.

So because love is dialogical then God as Love will also be so and his communicating with his beloved in order to share himself is not an optional extra which he can refuse to do but is his very nature. Thus the tradition of the Word of God in the Judaeo–Christian faith (the complexity of which cannot be examined in such a brief survey) focussing on Jesus the Word as the supreme revelation of God is perfectly consistent with, and indeed virtually demanded by, the belief that God is Love. The history of God's Word speaking to humanity stretches, of course, from Creation through the Old Testament covenant to its clearest pronunciation in the life, death and resurrection of Jesus and beyond that in the history of the church in the Holy Spirit. As with human lovers, the use of dialogue is made necessary because of the distinction between the two, and the Word of God although compelling in its declaration of love, respects that distinctiveness and does not coerce. It is a continual addressing and calling forth of his beloved humanity into a fuller selfhood which will be enjoyed in the reciprocal surrender in freedom and love to him. That this continual addressing and calling forth has eschatological implications ('the full self to be realized only in "becoming"') is evident not only because of the phenomenology of love, but because God's Word is so often addressed as a promise which simultaneously confirms his love and calls his beloved into further relationship. The use of the Word preserves not only the distinctiveness of the beloved but also of the lover, not only, therefore, of humanity but also of God. His transcendence is thus affirmed: Judaeo–Christian faith has expressed this in the statement that although humans have never seen God they have heard his word addressing them. Revelation is thus not only philosophically justifiable but consistent with the dialogical nature of love.

Love is also dialectical. God as Love, therefore, realizes his true self not only by possessing his beloved but also desiring to be possessed by her. In his great self-relatedness there is an even greater selflessness. Thus his turning towards humanity and sharing himself, giving himself away, apparently 'emptying' himself in becoming a human body and even becoming dependent upon human response is not, in fact, a denial nor losing of his divinity but a very manifestation of it. These attributes of love could not be made consistent with classical theism's understanding of the transcendence of God, but in the light of God's revelatory address to humanity and especially the event of the crucifixion and the resurrection of Jesus Christ, it becomes imperative that the understanding of transcendence should be re-defined.

The dialectical—dialogical nature of love is such that each partner can only find satisfaction in the Other – each I no longer wants to be an I without that Thou. In particular, the continuously dialogical nature of love is such that the beloved is continually 'called forth' by the influence, engagement with and care of the other so that although he remains distinct in their union he nevertheless becomes shaped by his beloved. That this happens in the relationship between God and humanity has usually been limited to the human pole of the partnership, i.e. humans who turn to God are said to grow in his image. Generally, however, no such statement has been made about God. Conceptually, it can be said that as love can be defined as 'within a great self-relatedness there is an even greater selflessness', so in the light of God's revelation of himself as a man in Jesus, 'for all his great dissimilarity, God is even more similar to humanity'.[11] The coming-to-be man, the apparent 'emptying' of himself, are yet more manifestations of his selflessness of love. Thus, the transcendence of God can be maintained in the sense of the separateness from humanity and in a redefinition of transcendence as selfless love rather than detached power.

However, this does not really solve our problem because of the way the word 'transcendence' has been used. So far it has been used as it could be used in any love relationship between humans: each partner is transcendent to the other in the sense that each is separate and the other is dependent upon her. However, such a use of the word does not solve the impasse because it raises the question whether God and love are not interchangeable in the sense that we can say that God is Love can be reversed to Love is God, thus deifying all human love and making even the use of the word 'God' a massive tautology, a tendency to which, it will be noted, Process theology is prone.

The true transcendence of God, the real affirmation of his divinity, and the real distinction between God and humanity is that he creates life. It is God alone who can create life 'out of nothing' as he did, not only at the beginning of history but also in the resurrection of the crucified Jesus from the dead. That event shows that God has identified himself with the life of that one man which was, itself, characterized by loving obedience to God's will. The resurrection has thus confirmed that God's will and love are one. In his commitment to humanity, God chooses to share in her life: this means making himself subject to contingent temporality and even to the negativities of human life, sin and death. These are profoundly alien to the life of the immortal, perfect God but are significant features of the life of humans which God has committed himself to share in love. Precisely because God is transcendent, there is nothing that he dare not face but because love makes a self vulnerable and open to being changed, he will be affected by and his self shaped by these things but, as the source of life, he cannot be overwhelmed by them. Having said that his power cannot be destroyed or matched, it must immediately be said that it cannot in any way deny or contradict his nature, which is Love. His power, then, cannot behave in anything but a loving way: it cannot coerce although it does compel.

It is to make this point strongly that this study climaxes in an exploration of the resurrection, emphasizing that the power which is there revealed is vulnerable love. For this reason, the resurrection (and by implication, the wider story of God's covenant with humanity) will be interpreted in the light of a love relationship between Jesus Christ and Mary Magdalene. Even more specifically, their story will be interpreted in the light of the marriage vow:

All that I am I give to you
All that I have I share with you,
Within the love of God Father, Son and Holy Spirit.

2

God as Lover:

Process Theology

The model for God as the cosmic Lover commends itself to us because it is religiously relevant, philosophically intelligible and scientifically acceptable. It tells us that God is to be seen as primarily Love-in-Act, who 'is what he does'; who is at work in the creation, who is 'time-full' since history matters for him and in him, who respects and values creaturely freedom and the responsibility which attaches to decisions made in that freedom, who is disclosed through his activity in nature and history but for Christian faith definitively in the man Jesus.[1]

If the claims which Norman Pittenger makes for Process theology can be substantiated it would appear that this particular school of modern theology satisfies the criteria needed to express both human and divine selfhood which were established in the opening chapter. It apparently preserves the human intellectual capacity because it takes seriously the developments in scientific and philosophical world-view, especially the theory of evolution. It also affirms human freedom and responsibility and acknowledges that the decisions which human beings make do actually affect the course of history. So important is human history and created reality that God is actually involved in it, not detached from it, as in classical theism. The value and dignity of creation and especially human beings are thus emphasized, and this points to an adequate appreciation of human personhood. The person of God is also in accordance with those criteria suggested in the previous chapter: God is active Love involved in creation and working for good, receiving into his life all which has been accomplished for good in history and working to transmute evils into occasions for further good.

This understanding of God derives its impetus from the person of Jesus whose life of love showed what God's nature is like. The primary feature of the God of Process theology is that he is a God of love and that love is characterized by the fact that he and human beings are involved in a partnership together in a way which the concepts of classical theism could not support. It is this idea of partnership which suggests the image of God as Lover to Pittenger. He expands his argument with a phenomenological description of love as it is experienced between human lovers: love involves commitment, mutuality, fidelity, hopefulness, communion, fulfilment and creativity.

That picture of human love, he suggests, can be paralleled to the love between God and creation. Such a direct parallel is possible within Process theology because it is one of its basic tenets that God is not to be seen as opposed to nature, a supernatural exception to the way in which the world works (as he was in Aquinas's Five Ways) but immanently present in the natural processes of the universe.

> God is not to be treated as an exception to all metaphysical principles but as their chief exemplification.[2]

The work of the Process theologians has been built on the philosophical theories of Alfred North Whitehead, whose metaphysics is an attempt to take seriously some of the developments in world view which have been outlined earlier. The metaphysic of Whitehead has since been adapted and modified into a Christian theology through the work of Charles Hartshorne and others.

As the name implies, Process thought takes seriously the

belief that the whole cosmos is in evolutionary process and
that God is involved in that process. This is, of course, a
departure from the classical picture of God, in which there
was no movement or change because movement was assumed
to be a feature of imperfection. It is, however, a return to a
more biblically-centred picture of God, for in the Judaeo–
Christian tradition God is actively involved in history. Process theology, then, seeks to take history and temporality
seriously. Yet Whitehead does not suggest that time is a
single, smooth flow but a series of distinct experiences which
are nevertheless fundamentally related so that they give an
impression of being continuous, rather as the separate frames
of a motion picture flow into each other so much that they
give the impression of being a continuous flow.

However, in spite of the name of the movement it is not
really process which is the most important feature of Process
theology. Perhaps of even more importance, and certainly of
more sigificance to this study, is the idea of the essential
relatedness of all things. The importance of this is indicated
by the fact that Whitehead called his philosophy 'a philosophy
of organism'. As in Einstein's Theory of Relativity, so in
Process thought, all things are interdependent not simply as
an ideal but as an ontologically-given characteristic. The
rigid distinctions between entities which was assumed in
Newtonian physics has been replaced by a complex interaction
between them. The religious significance of this is important.
To a large extent, the classical notion of God foreshadowed
the rigid divisions of the Newtonian picture. Certainly in
both any model of God showed him as totally independent
with no real relations to any other actuality. It was, therefore,
a logical procedure to argue that 'man made in the image of
God' should aim to emulate that independence. As has
already been stated, one of the important features of modern
theological thought, and one in which Process theology has
played a significant part, has been to show that such an
independent self-sufficient Being cannot possibly be described
as a God of Love.

The dependency of God

Hartshorne discerned another weakness in the classical model; a contradiction in its theory of the knowledge of God. Hartshorne argues that in both modern and mediaeval theory of knowledge, the knower is affected by what he knows, the subject is affected by the object and is dependent upon the object at least for the contents of that particular knowledge. 'Thus all roads seem to lead to the conclusion that the mind or awareness is the most relational or relative of all things.'[3] This theory of knowledge has however been reversed in classical theism in the understanding of God who is conceived of as knowing all things but with no dependence upon the thing that is known. Indeed, it is the creatures who are known who experience utter dependence upon him. Hartshorne is concerned to argue that the logic of knowing cannot be reversed like this in the case of divine knowing.

Furthermore, this reinforces his fundamental contention that the God of classical theism does not describe a God of Love. Arguing from the theory of relationships, he contends that to be in relationship any entity must, by definition, therefore, be in some way dependent upon the other things to which it is related. Again, that procedure has been assumed in terms of created reality but denid in terms of God. Hartshorne argues that dependency is not a sign of deficiency as has traditionally been assumed. Indeed, the reverse is true. A human being may become to be dependent upon another person in the sense that he needs that other person to fulfil his life. A dog may need its owner and may be said to experience something such as we would call 'love', although it could not be said to be comparable to human relationship. A stone is dependent upon no one. Yet it would be absurd to argue that the stone is therefore the highest entity of these three. Being related, and therefore being dependent to a certain extent is a sign of fullness of being rather than deficiency. It therefore follows, Hartshorne and other Process theologians argue, that to talk in terms of God being absolutely unrelated and independent is to imply a deficiency rather than perfection.

Hartshorne's concern is not simply a metaphysical matter of the theory of relationships and knowledge. He is concerned to do justice to belief in the contingency of the creation and in particular to the belief that it does matter what mankind actually does. For in the classical model of God, God remained unchanged by any human action and thus human freedom and choice were therefore nothing but an illusion. Creation and history were seen as a single, absolute world plan, complete in every detail from eternity and executed with inexorable power. It is this picture of God which has contributed to a denial of theism by so many in modern society because of its morally repugnant nature. Again, Hartshorne and many other modern theologians would argue that to deny that model is not to reject the Christian God, for 'how can anyone believe that being a follower of Jesus is like being an imitator of Aristotle's divine aristocrat?'[4]

The great difference between classical theism and Process theology is that in the classical model God's love is described as purely creative and not in any way dependent upon, or responsive to, the one who is loved. Process theology, on the other hand, takes human freedom and contingency seriously enough to draw a picture of God whose love is responsive to creation and to the decisions and activities of human beings.

The divine 'lure'

Again, whereas in classical theology God was seen as an autocratic controlling power in the universe, Process theology sees the divine creative activity as based upon responsiveness to the world. The argument runs that since the very meaning of actuality involves relatedness, God as an actuality is essentially related to the world and since the world is in a process of becoming which is, at least, partially dependent upon the self-creativity of the creature's decisions, future events cannot be determined in advance. So even God does not know the future and therefore cannot be said to control the world.

However, that does not mean that God simply allows the world to drift aimlessly. The fundamentally new conception of divine creativity, in Process thought, centres on the notion that God provides each worldly entity with an 'initial aim'. This means an impulse to actualize the best possible existence to fulfil itself. God gives to each creature that aim but because his nature is that of Love, he cannot force it to actualize its aim; the most that he can do is to persuade it. The outcome of this is to show, yet again, that God is not in complete control of events and therefore evil cannot be said to be God's will, but rather the result of creatures not choosing to fulfil that 'initial aim' intended for them.

Creation (by which Process theology always means continuing creation), is, in fact, a risk for God because he always takes the risk that his intention will be rejected. Thus in Process thought God is dependent upon creation to actualize itself. He can act as 'a lure' to it, drawing it closer to perfection by persuasion but he cannot enforce his intention. He can initiate novelty in the world although this does not come about in any interventionist manner (as in traditional theism) but it always continues with what has gone before. A changing order, inspired by God, expresses the evolution of creation.

> This means that the divine reality is understood to be the ground of novelty. This stands in tension with most religious philosophies, according to which deity ... is the ground of an established order. The God of Process thought is also the ground of order, but this is a changing and developing order, an order which must continually incorporate novelty if it is not to become repressive of enjoyment.[5]

However, it must be emphasized that this 'novelty' does not involve a break with the past because the space-time continuum is so tightly related that all things make up a 'seamless web' outside of which there is nothing. As each subject changes in its process of 'becoming' an experience may cause it to change direction and to look at its past experience through a different perspective so that it changes direction in the present and future. Indeed, it might feel to the experiencing subject that such a change has come 'from outside' and marks a definite break in its experience, but Process theologians would argue that such a change is continuous with the past.

The key to understanding this part of Process thought is that the building blocks of reality are seen to be not substances but events or occasions and thus a human person is composed of those past events of his experience which are then succeeded (in a strict continuity) by new events. Whitehead says that 'an enduring personality in the temporal world is a route of occasions in which the successors with some peculiar completeness sum up their predecessors'.[6] The key to personal identity is therefore inheritance and memory.

The fact that God intends that creation should be wholly loving but it does not live up to the perfection of that 'ideal aim' means that God himself is unfulfilled. However, that does not mean that God needs the world to be perfect before he can be God because God's love is always perfect (indeed it would cease to be perfect if he coerced the creation to fulfilment). As in a human relationship, one partner can love fully and the depth of that love is not lessened because it is not reciprocated, nevertheless a one-sided relationship or unreciprocated love does lack the fulfilment of a mutual love. So, in that sense God is dependent upon the world for his fulfilment.

The di-polarity of God

So far the picture that has been drawn is of a God who is wholly relative to the world, dependent upon it and sharing with it. The absolute nature of the classical concept of God has been altered completely. However, Process theology has also acknowledged the absoluteness of God by developing the concept of the di-polarity of God's nature: God has two poles to his nature, the relative (or consequent) and the absolute (or primordial). It was Whitehead who first proposed this although because of the vagueness of meaning it has been sharply modified by Hartshorne and later theologians.

Details of this concept vary from one thinker to another and all that can be given here is a simple outline and a discussion of the fundamental idea. The key to understanding this concept is the definition of human personality which has just been given: 'a route of occasions' created by all that has happened to the person. In Whitehead's system, all actual entities have two poles to their existence: the physical pole which is relative and immediate, and the mental pole which is the enduring personality, the sum of all that has happened in the past. Thus because in this system God is also an actual entity he also has these two poles. The relative or consequent is that by which he relates to the world and, as has been stated, is dependent upon the world. The absolute or primordial is his enduring personality, the sum of all that has happened to him in the past which, because he is God, means the sum of all that has happened. Anything which happens temporally is known and experienced by God and then, irrespective of how significant it was temporally, it passes into the absolute nature of God. So nothing in the whole of creation is ever 'lost' – it becomes part of the Godhead. That succession of past events then plays its part in influencing the present and the future as God continues to 'persuade' the universe towards fulfilment. So God is both an actual entity relating to the world and simultaneously an infinite succession of past experiences.

Panentheism

This di-polar notion of deity includes both the transcendent power and the humble gentleness of God and is, therefore, apparently an adequate expression of the selfhood of God. As has previously been noted, the Process model also defends the significance and dignity of human persons. Perhaps most significantly, however, this model offers an opportunity for speaking of a loving relationship between God and humans which classical theism, marked by a dualism of transcendence and immanence, found so difficult.

Responding to the theory of evolution by deriving an immanentist understanding of God's working in the actual events and processes of the world so that there is no part of the world where God is not active and present, Process theologians have nevertheless maintained the otherness of God and his transcendence over the world. So everything in the world is 'in God' but God's being is not exhausted by the world. This idea is called 'panentheism', and although not an idea limited to Process thought it is one which Process theologians have adopted into their schema:

> For the panentheist everything which is not itself divine is yet believed to be 'in God', in the sense that he is regarded as the circumambient reality in and through, while also more than, all that is not himself; or conversely, all which is not God has its existence within his operation and nature.[7]

This participatory model of God and humanity's activity and relationship has inspired the development of new ways of speaking about God and his love. To be more accurate, it has encouraged the re-discovery of images of God which have been neglected in the Christian faith under the domination of classical theism.

Perhaps the most significant and well known is the image developed by feminist theology of the motherhood of God. This picture accords with the panentheistic model because the baby is within the mother but yet the mother's being is not limited to that of the child's. They are inextricably entwined but yet they remain distinct.

There are, of course, many strands of both Process and feminist theology and it is, therefore, dangerous to generalize but it might fairly be said that these two schools of modern theology have found a partner in each other. Both would argue that the model of God traditionally presented in Western society '... is in many respects stereotypically masculine [in which he is] conceived to be active, unresponsive, impassive, inflexible, impatient and moralistic. This being had none of the stereotypically feminine traits ... it was not at all passive, responsive, emotional, flexible, patient and did not balance moral concern with an appreciation of beauty.'[8]

Further, they argue that because 'man is made in the image

of God' the understanding of God as held by human beings
is of great significance in human society because God's being
is mirrored in the self-understanding of humans and their
relationships with each other. Rosemary Radford Ruether
expresses the belief of many feminist and Process theologians
when she argues that

> the ultimate theological rationale for the hierarchical sym-
> bolism of masculinity and femininity is the image of God as
> transcendent Father. Creation becomes the wife or bride of
> the 'sky Father'. Most images of God in religions are
> modelled after the ruling class of society. In the Biblical
> religion the image of God is that of patriarchal Father above
> the visible, created world who relates to Israel as his 'wife'
> and 'children' in the sense of creatures totally dependent
> on his will, owing him unquestioning obedience. This
> image allows the king and patriarchal class to relate to
> women, children and servants through the same model of
> domination and dependence.[9]

In order to overcome this sanctioning of hierarchies of
domination new images of God need to be developed to
replace, or at least complement, the traditional images such
as Father, King and Lord. God as Mother incorporates an
appreciation of traits such as tenderness and patient, nurtur-
ing love and, above all, an inextricable physical unity of two
persons but the special value of the imagery of God as Lover
is that the two partners are seen as equals, needing one
another and enjoying one another. Indeed, the word 'lover'
might well avoid the implication of the traditional stereotype
of the husband as the head of the wife, noted by Ruether,
and in that sense is especially expressive of equality. Further,
because love involves compassion, a sharing-with the beloved
to the point of view of vulnerability, using this particular
metaphor avoids presenting him as impassive and unmoved
by the world's suffering.
   In so many ways, then, this picture rises to the criticisms
levelled against classical philosophical theism which were

advanced in the previous chapter, and presents a picture of the two persons of God and humanity which, while not physically united, as are mother and unborn child, are nevertheless bound together in a relationship of love so profound that it can be said to 'transform the beloved in her Lover'[10] and make them one.

Critique of Process theology

The aim of Process theology in responding to the criticisms levelled against classical theism is laudable and the picture of God which it draws does indeed appear to be more attractive than the 'monarchical' picture. It certainly takes as its central pivot the belief that Love is at the heart of the universe and it is easy to see why the picture of 'God as Cosmic Lover' most adequately expresses that model. However, before this picture can be seriously considered as an alternative (or even a complement) to the traditional images such as God the Father, it has to be recognized that there are many critical questions to be asked about it. These criticisms will be looked at now, examining them in terms of the internal logic of Process theology as well as measured against orthodox Christian doctrine and modern understanding of knowledge.

However, the criticisms arise from a fundamental dissatisfaction with the Process phenomenology of love especially in two aspects: vulnerability and particularity. It is my contention that Process theologians have tended to make two errors about the nature of love: they have equated vulnerability with passivity and they have assumed that love for one person in particular necessarily excludes the possibility of love for others. I will argue that such statements are not borne out by an observation of human love, and their inclusion in the Process theological scheme has resulted in a picture which fails to do justice to the love-relationship between God and his people, and the selfhood of both.

Passivity is not vulnerability

There can be very little question that Process theology has made an important contribution to the modern theological enterprise by its understanding of the relativity of God and its focussing of attention on human relationships in which 'love lets the other make a difference' has helped to make the conviction that 'God is Love' intelligible and meaningful. Of course, many other modern theologians who would not subscribe to the tenets of the Process model still assert the same characteristics of God, but this is not to deny the significant contribution made by Process theology in high-lighting the vulnerability and receptivity of God.

However, both observation of human love and reflection upon the picture of divine love portrayed in the Bible prompts a basic dissatisfaction with the Process understand-ing of the vulnerability of love. I would agree with Pittenger that:

> a basic difficulty in Christian theology has been and is, an inability to rest the case upon love. Somehow or other, it is felt that love must be backed up by force or there is no assurance of its triumphant quality[11]

but would argue that Pittenger and other Process theologians confuse any ability to act freely, exercising free will and initiative with coercive force. The God they have portrayed seems to be so concerned not to coerce the creation and destroy its freedom that, ironically, he has abdicated his own freedom to act. This passive God is thereby, apparently, less powerful than his creatures and thus hardly deserving of the adjective 'divine'.

Simple observation of human relationships suggest that such a pattern of behaviour would not merit the word 'love'. Love is *not* a completely unconscious, passive absorption by one partner but an active encounter in which they both give and receive. Of course there is an openness to receive but that receptivity is far more dynamic than the word 'passive' implies. In that openness to receive from each other each partner is transformed and transforms the other. Engage-ment with another in love means an opening of oneself to change and, indeed, to misunderstanding or rejection. It is this laying open of oneself to the other's influence and to the possibility of hurt and pain which is implied by the word 'vulnerability', a surrendering of one's own security in a risky fragility of encounter in which each partner is fully engaged and contributing their own personality and identity.

Passivity, on the other hand, implies an inability to act (or an unwillingness to do so) or be affected in any way. That element of dynamism between the two partners, that element of activity is missing if one partner is passive. Anything less than that dynamic exchange is not love. Such passivity implies that the full capabilities and identity of one partner – his freedom and conscious awareness in particular – are not fully engaged. It can actually become a form of detachment which can be its own defence mechanism against suffering and rejection. The whole tension between receptivity and activity, relationship and assertion of individual identity is far more complex than Process theology allows and I would suggest, is far more accurately and rigorously defined by the analysis of love outlined in the previous chapter, as a dialectical, dialogical mode of being in which the great self-relatedness is even more a great selflessness. In view of that, I would suggest that instead of speaking about 'receptivity' and 'acceptance' it would be appropriate to speak in terms of 'surrender' or 'giving' because those words imply an active element of conscious involvement. This justifies the controlling image of this entire work: the marriage vows in which two partners, far from being passive, actively and consciously surrender their selves to each other in vulnerable dependency.

Is God free to act?

However, it is not only observation of human love which makes questionable the picture of divine love as portrayed by Process theology. There are more fundamental conceptual problems, again centring on this idea of receptivity and relativity. Daniel Day Williams has summarized the basic convictions of many Process theologians when he writes:

I affirm that God does suffer as he participates in the ongoing life of the society of being. His sharing in the world's suffering is the supreme instance of knowing, accepting and transforming in love the suffering which arises in the world.[12]

The major criticism levelled against Process theology is that it is difficult to comprehend how God can actually be said to transform the world simply by sharing in it and empathizing with it. Indeed, it is difficult to see how he can act in any way at all and certainly questionable as to whether he is capable of taking any initiative. The internal logic of the Process system has apparently resulted in a God who is passive and that, as has just been noted, is far from being the same thing as vulnerable.

The key to this conception of God is that understanding of personality stated earlier in which a person is seen as 'a route of occasions' in which the present and future experiences sum up the previous ones. The fact that God is absolute and 'the chief exemplification of all metaphysical principles' means that he is conceived of as sharing in all that has ever happened and his personality consists of the memory of all happenings. This, for the Process theologian, is the Christian hope, the assurance of the eternal value and significance of human experience. Human beings (their personalities and activities) do not simply fade away, nor are they kept alive only in the memories of their human successors but what they have been and done is kept forever in the knowledge and being of God.

> because God's love, radically unlike ours, is pure and unbounded and because he therefore, both can and does participate fully in the being of all creatures, the present moment for him never slips into the past as it does for us ... all things are in every present quite literally resurrected or restored in his own everlasting life, from which they can never more be cast out.[13]

Similarly, Pittenger quotes with approval as 'good Process thinking' the poem by Richard Hovey in which a couple making love are given the guarantee that their joy will be forever a part of the divine joy.

God has said, Ye shall fail and perish
But the thrill you have felt tonight
I shall keep in my heart and cherish
When the worlds have passed into night.[14]

It is perhaps easy to appreciate why such a picture with its
sense of the omnipresence of God and its promise of vicarious
immortality to ensure the continuing value of each human
should be such an attractive alternative to the model of
classical theism. In process theology, 'God is in the cancer
and the sunset' and the dualisms which were found to be so
alienating in that previous model have been overcome. At a
simple level, the feeling that God can be experienced in
both joy and suffering is undoubtedly true but at a deeper
conceptual level this whole understanding raises many
serious questions about God's activity and freedom.

For a start, does the Process 'God' serve any purpose at all
in the sense that his nature and activity make any difference
to the world? Does he actually transform the world, as
Williams suggested, or does he simply act as the passive
recipient of the cosmic activity? Can he show any discrimination as to the goodness or badness of events in the world, or
must he simply absorb all that happens thereby conjuring up
a picture of a gigantic snowball, endlessly moving through
history, becoming ever larger as he assimilates more and
more experiences. If he simply does that, then God would
appear to be incapable of making any alterations or alternatively he must be condoning the world as it is already.

To be fair to Process theology, this impasse is largely a
result of Whitehead's very strict application of the idea of
dipolarity. Later Process theologians have themselves recognized the problem and tried to solve it by a greater flexibility
towards that conception. Hartshorne, for example, suggested
that God does not condone evil nor assimilate it into himself
but ignores it and thereby destroys it. Yet this raises more
questions than it solves. However many modifications and
clarifications are made there is a fundamental contradiction
which lies at the very heart of the Process conception of God

and I would argue that the foundations of the whole structure are such that there can be no possibility of resoloving the contradiction.

As has been remarked earlier, if any activity or engagement by God is conceived of as coercion then he cannot do anything other than absorb all that happens like 'a metaphysical sponge, infinitely absorbent'.[15] All that he can do is to empathize with his creatures (who are free to act) and share sympathetically in their suffering, suffering helplessly alongside them.

Indeed, God's freedom is so severely curtailed that it does seem that, in this system as much as in classical theism, the creation is trapped in an ultimate determinism. Process theology's determinism may be more subtle because here it is God who is determined by the decisions and activities of his creatures.

> The difficulty with the neo-classical suffering, for all its merits as a pointer to the real concern of God for his creatures is that it is not also a doing. It is totally automatic and involuntary. It is not under God's control for he has no choice whether or not he suffers with the world; in fact he is under the control of the cosmic forces which make him what he is.[16]

The distortion of seeing God in purely monarchical terms seems to have been replaced by an equally fatal distortion in the other direction. 'Instead of the Unmoved Mover (Hartshorne) has achieved the conception of an equally ineffective deity: the Moved Unmover.'[17] Further, not only is he as ineffective, he is as equally detached in that, as mentioned earlier, passivity constitutes a detachment from full involvement in a relationship.

The resurrection

Such is his passivity that it is hard to reconcile this picture with the biblical God who is actively and consciously engaged in a passionate relationship with his beloved people. It is just as difficult to reconcile with the biblical account of Jesus of Nazareth who, while he undoubtedly displayed the gentleness and persuasiveness so favoured by Process theologians, also displayed an active love which was so intensely passionate that he freely and consciously surrendered his own life in order to stay true to that love. The God of the Jewish and Christian scriptures (as revealed in Jesus) is both utterly loving and completely free to act, able to take initiative, free to involve himself in human history and natural processes yet not constrained by those processes. His nature and activity is far more passionate than anything conceived by Process theology.

Process theology's attempt to deny the omniscience of God does succeed in that limited aim, but it is unsatisfactory because then it falls into the trap of attributing a kind of omniscience to natural processes or at least to the human observer of those processes for it is possible to predict the future if, as Process thought argues, that future is rigidly predetermined by the past. Of course, human beings do not know the future but that fact is a statement about the present state of our knowledge. Within the logic of Process systematics it is possible to conceive of a time when the cause-and-effect of all things will be understood fully, and in that sense humans will be able to know the future. Once again, Process theology has drawn a model of God in which he is not as powerful as his creatures.

Perhaps even more seriously, it is a model which denies freedom either to God or humanity because both are trapped within a strict determinism of natural processes. In Process theology, God can apparently do nothing but receive what happens in the world and thus apparently he cannot initiate anything new. Even when he is described as the source of 'novelty' it is rather a misnomer because 'novelty' is in fact described as a repatterning of experience which is in direct continuity with the past.

This is hardly adequate to express the Christian conviction that God is actively involved in created history and source of life itself, not as the re-organizer of already existing entities. As such, it is inadequate to express the belief that in the resurrection of Jesus Christ, God acted within history in the same way as he had acted when he created the world, i.e. he created life out of nothing. In the resurrection, God performed an action which 'exploded' natural processes in a way which Process theologians could hardly countenance. Yet orthodox Christianity maintains that God must be accorded the freedom and power to create life itself if his true transcendence is to be recognized.

The model of Process theology is, within the limits of its own logic, adequately systematic in conceiving the principle of God's involvement with creation as self-sacrificing love climaxing in the crucifixion, but Process theologians notably find it difficult to accommodate the language of the resurrection into their scheme. One important book, for example, by John Cobb and David Griffin does not mention the resurrection of Jesus except in passing and the word does not even appear in the index. Other theologians, such as Pittenger, who is concerned to reconcile Process theology with traditional Christianity, do make more of it, but generally when Process theologians use such language it is in terms of the changed understanding of the experiencing person or within the memory of God.

The fundamental reason why the Process theologians cannot easily fit the resurrection into their scheme is because they confuse any direct action or taking of initiative as the exercise of force. Their instinct in avoiding the use of God as a *deus ex machina* who intervenes to sort out all problems may be sound but in so doing they have fallen into another error, that of conceiving God as utterly passive.

The way out of this impasse, I would suggest, is to emphasize that God's love is not passive but vulnerable, and that vulnerability is seen not only in the crucifixion (as Process theologians would emphasize) but also in the resurrection. If the fragile vulnerability of the resurrection can be appreciated then it becomes easier to see how this action which proclaims the priority and prevenience of God, his freedom and power to explode natural processes and create the genuinely new, does not necessarily have to destroy either the freedom of human beings or the loving nature of

God. It is for this reason that this study climaxes with the last chapter's interpretation of the resurrection as a vulnerable encounter of love between Jesus and Mary Magdalene.

First, however, there must be an examination of another major hesitation about Process theology: its lack of particularity and specificity.

Particularity does not exclude

The Easter encounter between Jesus and Mary Magdalene is also pertinent to this particular examination because this scene has been taken as suggestive of a more intimate, loving relationship than can be explained by a teacher-disciple relationship and has sometimes been interpreted as indicative of a particular love relationship between Jesus and Mary. The legend that Jesus and Mary Magdalene were lovers is widespread.[18]

This obviously cannot be proved and the question of historicity is not the most important question, in any case. Far more important is the consideration of one specific relationship of love between Jesus and another person and what that says about the nature of love. This idea of a relationship with Mary has posed problems in two main areas: the possibility of Jesus being involved in a sexual relationship (this will be examined later) and the idea of Jesus being involved in one special relationship, the implication being that if he is concerned with such a relationship he will not love others. In other words, particularity excludes.

This is the phenomenology of love assumed by Process theology which is so concerned to show that God is in all things ('in the cancer and the sunset') and loves all things that it apparently cannot accommodate any idea of a specific relationship with one particular person. This, in itself, stems from the difficulty of conceiving of the distinctiveness of a person at all. It is interesting to note, for instance, that Pittenger's picture of God as Lover is unusual in Process theology because it actually does conceive of God in personal terms. Other terms applied to God are neutral: 'Love-in-Act',

'Loving Activity in the World', or even 'God as Verb'.[19]
Ironically, the very movement which attempts to picture a
more intimate, less alienating God has resulted in such
impersonal descriptions. This lack of personal definition of
God is reflected in the description of humans in similarly a-
personal terms which lacks specificity and historical realism.
This means that it is extremely doubtful whether Process
theology can do justice to the Incarnation and the specific life
of one historical person as the supreme revelation of God.
Cobb and Griffin's comment on Whitehead is noteworthy.

> His comments express Whitehead's deep impression of
> Jesus and respect of his authority. He leaves open the
> equal importance of analogous events occurring elsewhere.
> But he does hold that Plato's insight and Jesus' life embody
> the greatest advances in the expression of moral 'intuitions
> which mark the growth of recent civilization'. Because of
> Jesus' embodiment of a supreme ideal 'the history of the
> world divides at this point of time'.[20]

Admittedly, there are other quotations in which Jesus is
spoken of as the decisive revelation of God and to quote
these would give the impression that full appreciation of the
significance of Jesus is made by the Process theologians. It
would, however, be just that – an impression. There is about
the language of Process theology 'a studied vagueness'
which makes it difficult to criticize and yet leaves the serious
reader with the feeling that it lacks sufficient decisiveness
and substance.

Objectivity of form
However, while acknowledging such vagueness there is no
reason for it to become contagious! It may be difficult to cite
short passages out of context, but it is possible to trace the
vagueness to the overall cosmological framework employed
by Process theologians in their concern to emphasize the
relatedness of all things. So strong is their emphasis on this
interconnectedness that they are afraid to assert individual
identity and distinctiveness lest that should detract from the

unity. Such a fear is not only unnecessary but might well be argued to be philosophically anachronistic because it depends too much on the Newtonian world view, a question which will be examined fully in the next chapter.

Here, there is only space to refer to the ideas of Einstein and quantum physics which have made it possible for some interpreters to conceive of the world as a complex nexus of specific but inter-related realities which are continually reacting with and responding to each other in such a way that there can be no prior determination or knowledge of the results of such reactions. The most that can be offered is a considered guess based on observation of similar reactions in the past, but since every single entity is unique and every moment in time also unique there can be no guarantee that the results will be the same as they have always been in the past. Creation is thus not the closed order of cause and effect posited by Newton and adopted, if somewhat indirectly, by Process theologians. Rather it is an open order in which chance, freedom, contingency and probability are built into the very nature of reality. The appropriate response to such a created order has therefore to be open and flexible, ever prepared to discover new things and indeed to be surprised and amazed by the possibility of something completely new happening.

Another way of expressing this is to emphasize the objectivity of each entity: objective not in the sense of being detached from other forms, but in the sense that as each form is unique it must be 'other' than other forms and cannot ever be contained by any other form. Each entity must allow the other to be true to its own identity, the development of which cannot be predicted or manipulated.

In purely theological terms such cosmology offers the possibility of speaking about God as objective in that he cannot be contained but reveals himself in ever new ways to his human partners who respond in openness and wondrous amazement at these new things. Conversely, it means that as God has created a world of contingent freedom he will himself be continually open to, and surprised by, what humanity decides and becomes. Process theologians had intuited that if God was truly to be defined as in loving relationship with free human beings, then he must become dependent upon them and lose his omniscience and omnipotence in the sense that he cannot know and control the future. As has already been argued, the logical outworking of their system has resulted in God being denied any kind of real power and his knowledge is limited to that of a passive observer. The loyalty of Process theology to a Newtonian closed system of natural laws has meant that it could not press its intuition as far as it becomes possible to do in an Einsteinian world view: in this God can be conceived of as genuinely surprised by the developing of the world, genuinely unable to dictate the future and yet still attributed with the power appropriate to divinity.

Conceptually, the picture which emerges both in this section and the previous discussion of the active and full engagement of two partners is the kind of relationship defined in the first chapter, a relationship of two partners who see each other as an I. Of course, that discussion expands the idea of the dialectical–dialogical nature of love expressed in addressing, calling-forth and turning-to the other. All of these are subsidiaries to the central love in a relationship between two 'I's: it should not be necessary, therefore, to make a detailed, point-by-point comparison between that conceptualization of love and Process theology because it is very difficult to see how Process theology, with its passivity and vagueness, can ever conceive of such a relationship.

That lack of definition also means that although the fundamental concept of Process theology is the flow of history, the word 'overflow' (our fundamental definition of love) cannot really be applied to its world because that, as has been argued previously, implies a 'flowing-out of' and 'a flowing between' distinct entities.

Indeed, in spite of the use of words such as 'novelty' and 'adventure' the world described by Process theology seems unexciting, monochrome and (perhaps literally) predictable.

Its inability to allow for specificity of form and its adherence to rigid natural laws cannot allow for the endless variety of form which characterizes the created universe:

> Such subtle intelligibility or such immense wealth of form, defying the possibility of final formalisation, would not characterise the universe if it were ultimately necessary, for necessity at the back of everything would only stereotype or standardise all patterns in nature and what a dull universe that would be.[21]

Compared to the world conceived of in the opening analysis of love in which superlatives are stretched to breaking point by the experience which is best evoked in the words 'more than', Process theology's creation does indeed seem static and prosaic. Just the kind of dull universe which Torrance warned against.

The scandal of particularity

On the other hand, if the picture of reality is one in which multivarious, particular, definable forms are in continual relationship with each other, the possibility then arises of being able to speak, for example, about the uniqueness of the person of Jesus Christ in a way which does not imply that if God is uniquely involved in Jesus he cannot be involved with others. This opens the possibility of speaking in terms of 'the scandal of particularity' which lies at the heart of the Christian faith: that God has chosen one man and one people to be particular agents of his will and participators in his love without excluding his love for others.

It is this 'scandal of particularity' which leads to the conclusion that the image of 'God as Lover' is not concrete and specific enough to do justice to God's love. Although in reality there can be no simple assumption that the love of a married couple is any deeper than that of the unmarried, the analogy of God as Husband does at least imply a specific and disciplined commitment to one other individual in a way the word 'lover' need not. Love, I would contend, is directed towards a specific Other although such a specific love does not actually exclude others, but by increasing the loving capacities of the partners actually enables them to love more widely. That love is not only directed towards another but involves disciplined commitment and rigorous application.

Daniel Hardy's reflection on the life and theology of Paul Tillich has much to say to Process theology also:

> Consider Hannah Tillich's account of his behaviour at a party shortly after their marriage. 'He had left me often, flirting with other women, leaving each one in turn for another at the succeeding dinner party. I had to take care of the spurned one who came to me shamelessly complaining about Paulus' unfaithfulness, which amused me.'

Tillich's fascination with each woman was an affirmation, but only occasional and short-lived, in which each was 'left in turn' – apparently because of the hidden premise that the excitingly hidden and the new were intrinsically better ... And Tillich's theology reflects this occasionalism lacking any element of loyal perseverance. 'On the one hand, God (is) seen as an ultimately unspecifiable ground of being ... and on the other hand, the activity of life and faith ('accepting that you are accepted') bespeaks an off-and-on activity in which loyalty and constancy are never achieved.'[22]

The Bible tells the story of God's relationship with humanity in terms of the covenant (at times explicitly invoking the analogy of the marriage covenant) and it does seem appropriate use that analogy to express the nature of God's constant and disciplined love, not exclusively for his initial covenant partners but as an indication of the nature of his love for all. The imagery of marriage keeps to the fore God's freedom and will.

However, if we are to apply the characteristics of love listed in the opening chapter consistently, then the significance of love towards a specific Other must be pressed further. In that list the gracious nature of love was mentioned: love is awakened and aroused by the Other not because of any special merit or virtue on her part but purely gratuitously, i.e. the lover does not decide beforehand that it would be a good idea to fall in love with that particular one rather than any other. The turning to – and responsibility towards the Other – comes as a response to being awakened by the Other. Love towards the specific Thou involves free will and choice and in that sense the lover is active. Yet it also involves dependency upon that Thou, a dependency which is so radical that the self's whole life and identity must be re-orientated (or better still *is* re-orientated) so that the Thou, rather than the I, becomes the primary criterion for that self's life. In that sense, the lover is passive (the word is grossly inadequate and is only used as the opposite of 'active' to communicate the essential paradox of what is being described): he does not choose but feels compelled towards that Other in such a way that he might well say that he feels 'chosen'. Thus, in love, the self is freely and fully engaged (a great self-relatedness) but that self which is fully engaged only wants to live away from itself towards the Other, to surrender and lose its own self, to be ex-centric in that even greater selflessness which is the nature of love.

The freedom and choice of God in relation to loving a particular people has already been mentioned but if the other aspect of this conceptualization of love is also applied, then God's love for a specific people can be seen as a response to that beloved herself, but not because she is necessarily different, better or more suitable than any other. So, the question can be asked, 'Why did God choose Israel as his covenant partner?' and the answer be given, 'No obvious and special reason.' Similarly, it might be asked, in relation to the theme of this book, 'Why did Jesus fall in love with Mary Magdalene and not, say, Martha?'

As in any human relationship, there may be a partial explanation in such things as shared interests but there can never be a full answer because many couples who seem theoretically 'meant for each other' never share that compulsion of self-giving love which is being discussed. Conversely, others who apear to be a most unlikely couple manifestly experience that utter conviction of love. Love is that gratuitous, that mysterious and uncontrollable. This understanding which may assist to avoid any idea that God chose Israel because of any extra merit on her part, is the traditional idea of 'being called by grace alone'.

Here the concern is not so much with the experience or merit of God's beloved Israel but with thinking through 'radically and consistently' what this understanding of love says about God. Traditionally, teaching about God's grace has been used to defend the freedom of God even to the point of emphasizing his detachment. However, if this conceptualization of love is applied, then God's gracious relationship with Israel rather than with any other nation can be viewed through a different perspective: if God is to be involved in a world of contingency, then his love might very well be awakened by one particular people rather than by another. In that arousal of love, he chose freely to commit himself to that one but the activity of his choosing and committing is already circumscribed by that compulsion towards the Other, before whom he might be said to be 'passive' or obedient. Traditional teaching has not pressed thus far because of the fear of denying God's power and control. However, if that power is radically defined as selfless love which freely relinquishes itself, surrendering control into the hands of the Other who has aroused that love, then God's power is not thereby denied.

Such a conclusion must be applied extremely carefully and is limited in its relevance. It cannot be applied to 'the scandal of particularity' in terms of the life of Jesus because God's involvement in that life is more complex and thorough, not so much a relation *with* an Other but being *in* an Other; such complexity is traditionally defined in terms of the 'hypostatic union' rather than 'covenant' and will be explored as such in later chapters. It is, similarly, unsatisfactory in terms of the church as a chosen people because that involves a recognition of God's activity and presence in the life of Jesus of Nazareth. This also will be examined in detail later.

However, while acknowledging the limits of its applicability, it can be applied to the call of Israel and, for example, to the call of the disciples. *Fundamentally, it is a statement that the*

*grace of God implies not only his freedom to choose but the freedom
also to be limited and dependent.*

It is such another expression of the basic conviction of this
work that in being self-giving and self-effacing God is not
denying his true nature but actually fulfilling it. If the utterly
loving God is to be actually involved in the contingent world
then he will be limited and the argument of these past
paragraphs sows seeds of ideas which will be picked up later:
the limitations freely accepted by God in the Incarnation, the
redefinition of transcendence as a humility which involves
'looking up to' the other whose objectivity and value is thus
preserved.

Of course, if that conceptualization of love is applied to
one pole of the relationship it must be done also to the other
partner: if love is aroused mysteriously and graciously by the
human partner through no special merit, cannot the same be
said of the divine? In other words, 'Why this God and no
other?' This is, of course, the question demanded by the
pluralist nature of our society and which must be answered
satisfactorily if the whole of the human person (including the
intellect) is to be engaged in the relationship.

The key to the answer lies in the word 'God': the task of
the one who seeks to answer this question is to indicate that
the one who is revealed in Jesus Christ is truly God and truly
transcendent, i.e. that he is the creator of life itself. That is to
say, the question does not ask 'Why this source of comfort
rather than that?', 'Why this source of inspiration rather than
that?', 'Why not this good man instead of Jesus?' If the
question was simply at that level, then Christianity would
indeed be one among many options. However, the question
really focusses on indicating that Jesus Christ reveals the
only God that there is, the Creator of Life.

Summary

In spite of the criticisms levelled against Process theology, a
wholesale dismissal of its ideas is not intended. The hesita-
tions which it has intuited about the classical notion of
God are accepted and echoed in this work. However, its

conceptual framework has been argued to be unsatisfactory particularly in terms of activity and specificity. Nevertheless, some of its key insights (e.g. the vulnerability of God, the significance of human beings to God, the interconnectedness of all things and the flow of history) will be integrated into what is intended to be a more rigorous conceptualization which is, in fact, that of orthodox biblical Christianity. The ideas which Process theology has rejected are not those of orthodox Christianity but classical theism. Orthodox Christianity, on the contrary, offers the possibility of speaking about God and humans in precisely the kind of relationship which we are working towards: in which the perfectly loving God surrenders himself to free human beings in a relationship of mutual trust which yet does not deny his real transcendence.

3

Knowing and Loving:

Questions of Knowledge

The opening chapter listed various components which needed to be included in an adequate definition of human selfhood. One of these was intellectual reasoning and it was remarked that since the Enlightenment this has been one of the most significant contributory factors to the decline of religious faith. Consequently, any serious exploration of the Christian faith must face up to the question of how it is possible to speak of faith in God without denying the faculty of human reasoning. In other words, the question must be asked, 'How can God be known?' and the answer sought within the concepts and categories of human understanding. Otherwise it cannot be said satisfactorily that human intellect is involved in any relationship with God. On the other hand, as the first chapter proceeded to argue, any discussion of human self must be complemented by a discussion of the divine self which must acknowledge his transcendence. If God is transcendent then he cannot be known as if he were just another object. The fundamental question may well be expressed thus: how is it possible to conceive of God who is beyond human knowing?

Epistemology, the question of how human beings 'know', is so vast and complex that one chapter cannot possibly claim to range over the many ideas and answers given to the subject of the knowing of God. The aim of this chapter is

simply to indicate that the ideas and concepts developed in
the rest of this work (such as 'turning to the Other', the
scandal of particularity, promises, commitment and the process of becoming) can be argued to be valid epistemological
principles. We will, in fact, be continuing our 'radical and
consistent' application of the declaration that God is Love to
the question of human knowing, arguing that the resolution
of the paradox 'How is it possible to know God who is
beyond human knowing?' can be found (as in the biblical
equation of love and knowledge) in the primacy of love.

Knowledge as 'turning to the other'

Since the Enlightenment, questions of knowledge have tended
to be dominated by a dual emphasis on the knowing subject,
the I, and also on the need for proving any contention of
truth within the framework of strict natural laws. The language about knowing has thus assumed an objective observer
rationally analysing the properties of the world as they exist
independent of his observations.

Such a view is no longer tenable: modern physics (especially
the relativity and quantum theories) has helped to precipitate
a revolution in thinking, dismantling the rigidities of absolute
space and absolute time in Newtonian physics and replacing
them with a complex space-time continuum. The universe is
thus no longer believed to act according to strict natural laws
which had the effect of clamping everything down into a
hard deterministic or mechanical structure, but is seen as an
ever open and expanding system of contingent realities and
events encountering one another.

The very contingent nature of these realities means that,
by definition, each one is unique. Thus in order to understand
each one, attention and respect must be paid to that uniqueness rather than assuming that they will be and will behave
like other similar beings. Every form and every event is
unique and unrepeatable, yet in the interconnectedness of
the space-time continuum they do not exist in splendid
isolation and detachment from other forms (as Newtonian
physics tended to assert) but are connected with and

encounter other forms, equally unique and unrepeatable. Again, the contingency of the universe means that there can be no prediction as to precisely what encounters will occur and therefore what new forms, beings and relationships will emerge.

Furthermore, the complexity of understanding is intensified by the encounter between each objective reality and the observer who is himself an objective entity and thus brings his own self to the act of observation and understanding.

> Man cannot describe the physical world as if his own investigations had no effect on it; especially at the level of the individual atomic processes, the scientific observer has a role in creating the world he is describing by his mere act of observation. We are both onlookers and actors in this great drama of existence.[1]

So great has been the revolution in thinking caused by the relativity theory that a new way of looking at the world and a new language for speaking about it still needs to be established. Part of the contention of this study is that somewhat mechanical language which has predominated as a way of describing the world must be complemented by the language of relationships which can express the complexity and simplicity of the way in which humans understand the world.

Knowing as encounter

Several modern philosophers have sought to establish such a world-view and language for the 'post-liberal' or 'post-critical' culture. Hans Georg Gadamer, for example, suggests that the nature of understanding is analogous to a conversation, and his examination is clearly reminiscent of our characterization of love.

In *Truth and Method*,[2] Gadamer considers various ways of engaging a person in conversation. The first way is not really a conversation at all because the other person is merely another object to be observed, categorized and his behaviour predicted. Such observations aim to achieve an objective knowledge but such objectivity denies the personhood of the one who is being observed.

Another kind of conversation is that which passes between a counsellor and her client in which one person witholds her own personhood from the conversation in order to focus on the other person. The client's own personhood is here recognized but the counsellor's own self is not fully engaged in the relationship. This is another form of detachment and although there may be occasions when such a relationship is wholly appropriate, it must be acknowledged that such a conversation is open to the possibility of the counsellor manipulating the client while in no way allowing herself to be vulnerable.

The third type of conversation suggested by Gadamer is one in which the individual person not only recognizes the otherness of the other person but also recognizes his claim over her, listening to what he has to say without trying to dominate him or control him. It is genuine listening and genuine openness to each other. This third type of conversation corresponds to our definition of a loving relationship in which two 'I's participate together in a dynamic of mutual addressing and calling-forth of their respective selfhoods; in other words, it corresponds to the model of dialectical–dialogical mode of being.

This discussion points us towards the possibility of speaking about knowledge as love: the way in which a person comes to know something is similar to the way in which he engages in a loving relationship with another human being. In love the self is re-defined through encountering the other and the loving self thereafter does not want to be that I without that particular Thou.

In a similar way, if the knowing self encounters any other (be it person or inanimate object) then his mind may be closed in the sense that he refuses to receive any new knowledge and be changed by the encounter. Alternatively, he can be prepared to receive new truth from that other in that other's objective integrity and independence. In other words, he will be open to receive whatever that other has to offer and once that has been done the knowing I has been changed and he can no longer be the I that he was previous to this encounter.

This applies as much to, say, scientific experiments (in which the scientist must be prepared to receive whatever results occur and must not close his mind in the sense of pre-determining the result in accordance with the dictates of previous knowledge) as it does to personal relationships. It applies to knowledge which is obviously cerebral; the student who fully engages himself in the elaborate conceptual argument of a lecture which he is attending will henceforth be a changed person and no longer able to approach his future studies without referring to those newly understood concepts.

It applies also to non-cerebral knowledge such as the impression left upon the imagination by a dream which enables the knowing self to view her own self and the world in a new way. Indeed, it applies to all the knowledge gained by a person: as in the characterization of love so this epistemological conceptualization asserts that the self is not a pre-social static entity but one who is what she is only through being in relationship.

Personal knowledge

Another post-critical philosopher, Michael Polanyi, has termed this idea of epistemology as 'personal knowledge': this transcends the distinction between subjective and objective knowledge in the sense that as 'the personal submits to requirements acknowledged by itself as independent of itself it is not subjective but in so far as it is an action guided by individual passions it is not objective either'.[3]

Personal knowledge according to Polanyi is a 'turning-towards' the other, turning away from ourselves and acknowledging its independent reality and truth. A person thus acts rationally when she does not confuse reality with herself. The problem with mysticism, animism, pantheism (and that to which Process theology is prone) is that the knowing self is not adequately distinguished from the object which she knows.

Knowledge in Polanyi's understanding is a kind of listening obedience of the mind to reality, a basic act of recognition
in which our minds respond to a pattern or structure inherent
in the world around us which imprints itself upon them,
whether that pattern be the results of scientific experiment or
the personality of a human being. That pattern cannot be
predicted because in a contingent world all entities are
utterly unique.

It is this acknowledgement of the reality and rationality of
'the other' which prevents knowledge from falling into pure
subjectivism, for the mind must recognize the reality of the
independent object as it is 'in itself'. There is thus a certain
compulsion about the way something is known arising from
the fact that its intelligible structure is dictated by its own
nature and not by the arbitrary fancy of the observer. The
knower is compelled to acknowledge the distinctiveness of
the object because he feels that this is the only appropriate
response to something which he encounters beyond himself.
He is thus compelled to acknowledge the 'givenness' of that
reality.

However, that compulsion is not to be interpreted as
coercion in the sense that what is known is forcibly impressed
on human minds, because that would be a denial of the
independent reality and freedom of the knowing self. Like
the object, the subject or knowing self is also an independent
reality whose distinctiveness must be preserved and affirmed
and that means that its choice whether to respond or not to
the 'givenness' of another reality must be preserved.

Polanyi argues that to know something to be true is to
commit oneself to the implications of that knowledge as 'true
for you', although there can be no absolute proof of its truth.
It is the frame of mind 'in which I may hold firmly to what I
believe to be true even though I know that it might conceivably be false'.[4] Commitment to one particular belief (the
word is used for all forms of knowledge, not only the
religious) is not a denial of the freedom of the knower but
actually an affirmation of it.

Polanyi uses the example of a judge deciding on a test case

by narrowing down the range of options to one and thus showing the power of his responsibility over himself. 'This is his independence: the freedom of the subjective person to do as he pleases is overruled by the freedom of the responsible person to act as he must.'[5]

I would suggest that another excellent expression of this paradox is the attitude assumed at the exchange of marriage vows made in freedom yet under the compulsion of what might be termed 'the necessity of love'. Marriage vows, like legal test cases, are vulnerable and risky: there can be no absolute guarantee that the right decision has been taken, yet there is simultaneously a certainty that no other decision is possible. This paradoxical mixture of freedom and obligation is superbly summarized in the famous declaration of Luther, 'Here I stand, I can do no other.'

Indwelling

So the process of knowing can be seen to be very similar to the process of loving. Just as the loving self can only be truly herself with her beloved, so the knowing self cannot be the person she was before she learned that new knowledge. Similarly, as the loving self comes to share her selfhood in the self of the other so that the two cannot be clearly divided, so the new knowledge which is acquired becomes part of the very self of the knower. This is what Polanyi means by personal knowledge: knowledge which is not simply subjective because it has been achieved by a disciplined submission to the objective reality of the 'other' but which has nevertheless been intrnalized so that it can be said to be the knower's own.

In Polanyi's definition such knowledge is an 'indwelling'. He uses examples from the performance of skills, the proper use of the sensory organs and the mastery of tools to show that to know something does not mean a detached observation of that thing but a participation in it. A learner driver may be able to quote the text book exactly but the experienced driver, who has reached the stage of reacting spontaneously and probably could not explain how he responded to a situation, will be more likely to be the better driver – he can be said to 'indwell' his car and his knowledge of driving technique.

Polanyi argues that we also indwell language: words and concepts are more than a detached observation of reality, they are the means by which human beings actually participate in reality. So, for example, a child learning a language or an adult learning a second language accepts from the community to which the language 'belongs' the meanings indicated by that language and makes them his own. He 'indwells' that language. Knowledge as love, then, is a dialectical mode of being in which the I receives his identity through participating in that which is other to himself. 'In knowledge as in all else he labours in vain to be independent: he is most himself when he receives most, and most freely acknowledges that he receives.'[6]

Polanyi uses the idea of 'indwelling' to describe entering into an intimate relationship with something or someone in which the whole life of the person concerned is involved. It therefore involves commitment and that not just for the immediate moment but for the future as well. In scientific examination, for example, Polanyi argues that it is appropriate to use the term 'natural law' about some reactions because out of the very many possibilities for the behaviour of matter scientists have decided to commit themselves to that one particular way of understanding truth. However, that commitment must always be tempered by the humble acknowledgment that new discoveries will prove that 'law' to be no longer applicable and needing to be replaced by another. 'To hold a natural law to be true is to believe that its presence may reveal itself in yet unknown and perhaps unthinkable consequences; it is to believe that natural laws are features of reality which as such will continue to bear consequences inexhaustibly.'[7]

The language of testimony

Knowing and loving both involve the future. The bridal couple commit themselves to each other for the future, convinced that their participation in one another will continue throughout the changes and developments of their contingent lives. They cannot know how the future will turn out, their marriage is an act of faith and hope. Similarly, in knowledge no person can know what he will come to know and become. In his life he will encounter many people and many events. From his engagement with these others he will change and grow so that his knowing self can only be described as 'becoming'. In order to express what a person is her life story must be told to clarify the influences and circumstances which have made her indwell the particular knowledge which she now has. Each person's knowledge will 'be true' for him while at the same time being contingent, fallible and partial because there can be no absolute arbiter of truth as a universal norm.

None of this is to discredit the faculty of disciplined, critical thought although it is to argue the severe limitations of the excessively critical stance of much post-Enlightenment society in which there has been a suspicious rejecting of receiving traditional knowledge and in which the emphasis has been on proving something to be true before it can be believed. Even when it is recognized that there is more to understanding than simply an intellectual process, disciplined critical thinking is appropriate, not least because it is by such discipline that new stages of understanding are reached.

In a mature love relationship the couple need not fear questions about their relationship. It may well be that family and friends who are on the outside might see questions which need to be asked and a mature, secure relationship might very well be strengthened by heeding these questions. However, for those questions to be effective they must be appropriate to that relationship. Questions which would be appropriate to ask when faced with a sheet of accounts would not be the right ones to ask at the exchange of marriage vows. The attitude behind a particular question is also significant: it might well be circumspect for a white father to ask questions about his son's intended marriage to a black woman, on the grounds of possible future problems precipitated by a clash of culture. That might be wise and the couple, in being made to face such issues, might very well grow. If, however, such questions are raised out of racial prejudice they are not appropriate: because only a loving response is appropriate to love. Similarly, it might well be wise to remind a person of the reason for the breakdown of a previous relationship 'in case the same thing happens again'. Yet to assume that it is bound to happen again is to ignore the sheer particularity, the uniqueness of this relationship and such a question is therefore inappropriate.

Further, only those who are participating in the relationship can know its truth and rightness for them. A couple who decide to marry are basically saying (and not just in words), 'We can appreciate all the reasons for doubt and hesitation (financial considerations, previous breakdowns in relationship, future problems) but when all is said and done we know that we love one another.' It is the language of testimony, just as a Christian believer says, 'I can understand all the questions which are raised about my beliefs (that it is wish-fulfilment, projectionism etc) but when all is said and done, I know that my Redeemer lives.'

The language of revelation

The correspondence between this modern epistemology and traditional Christian teaching should by now be quite obvious. The doctrine of God's revelation of himself and the human's humble obedience to it is saved from a crude naivety when it is argued that such a humble obedience is a reasonable epistemological category applied to all forms of human knowing.

Similarly, the individual's immersion in the wider, corporate body of the church is seen not as an abrogation of independence but the dialectical mode of being in which the self is truly fulfilled. Within this understanding, even a statement such as the dictum of Cyprian of Carthage that 'outside the church there is no salvation' becomes comprehensible as a recognition of mutual dependence rather than myopic prejudice. Again, another traditional Christian principle is that 'faith seeks understanding' rather

than understanding generates faith and this assumes re-
newed relevance in Polanyi's discussion of knowledge
involving participation. He quotes Isaiah's words to illus-
trate this principle, 'If you will not believe you will not
understand.'

The temporal element is also relevant to the Christian
faith. Just as people 'become' over a period of time they
indwell in their expanding knowledge so God's relationship
with the world can only be told as a story of a conversation
between two partners, both of whom address and call forth
the other's emerging selfhood.

> A two way movement was involved: an adaptation of
> divine revelation to the human mind and an adaptation of
> articulate forms of human understanding and language to
> divine revelation. That is surely how we are to regard
> God's long historical dialogue with Israel: the penetration
> of the Word of God into the depths of Israel's being and
> soul in such a way that it took human shape and yet in
> such a way that the human response which it called forth
> was so locked into the Word of God that it was used as the
> vehicle of further address on the part of the Word to
> Israel.[8]

This discussion of the dialogue between God and humanity
will be continued in the next section. Here a summary of this
section is made which concludes that:

1. Knowledge is acquired through turning to the other and
receiving what the other has to give.

2. Knowledge involves participation in that other's identity
in the sense that your self can no longer be complete without
that other.

3. Knowledge is a process of becoming.

To know something is to participate in it and to allow it to
participate in your self. To know God, therefore, is to
participate in him and since he is Love that means to
participate in love, sharing his nature of utterly constant,
self-giving love which cannot withhold itself but must give of
itself freely and joyfully.

The traditional Hebrew equation of the words 'to know' and 'to love' become even more meaningful because as we have defined knowledge it is both a respect for the objectivity of the other ('turning to' it) and a participation in it both of which are attitudes displayed in our characterization of love.

The promising God

This section takes the epistemological question further because it is still necessary to clarify how it is possible to speak in terms of any exchange between God and humanity (which implies their equality) and still maintain the idea of God's prevenience without which any idea of divinity would be diminished. The analogy of a human love relationship is useful to a certain degree in expressing the relationship between God and humanity, but such a relationship becomes inappropriate if the absolute equality of both partners is assumed; in our relationship with God there is an asymmetry because we are utterly dependent upon him for existence as no human being is ever so dependent upon a lover.

Part of the reason for the failure of the scheme of Process theology, I would suggest, is that its emphasis on the mutuality and partnership militated against any appreciation of this asymmetry. This failure helped to produce the ineffective Deity helplessly tied up with the processes of creation. Process theology could not allow for any kind of deviation from usual epistemological rules, yet traditional Christianity has maintained that God cannot be known as if he were just another created object. In line with this traditional teaching, T. F. Torrance has written:

> In all our knowing it is we who know, we observe, we examine, we inquire but in the presence of God we are in a situation in which He knows, He observes, He examines, He inquires and in which He is 'indissoluble subject'. This relation in which the ultimate control passes from the knower, who yet remains free, to God who is known in His knowing of us is an important aspect of what we call faith. Faith is the relation of our minds to the Object who

through His unconditional claims upon us establishes the centre of our knowing in Himself and not in us, so that the whole epistemological relation is turned round – we know in that we are known by Him.[9]

It has been previously noted that in order for God 'to be God' he must be credited with the freedom and capacity to initiate the genuinely 'new thing', to create *ex nihilo* and raise from the dead. Such a capacity for the creation of life demands that asymmetrical relationship between God and human beings who, while having many capabilities, cannot actually create life.

Yet simply to assert an epistemological inversion is still to avoid the problem of how it is possible to speak of any kind of relationship and dialogue between God and humanity because it avoids using human conceptuality and categories of understanding. To argue that God reveals himself in a way which does not have to be justified in terms of ordinary human rationality is to deny the full engagement of the human person in this relationship and therefore to fall into the same dangers and problems as the traditional theistic model which were outlined in the introductory chapter.

I have no intention of giving a detailed analysis of the work of Torrance and therefore it is unfair to quote isolated passages without giving a full appreciation of the subtleties of his arguments. However, while recognizing that this work has been important in pointing the way forwards for a reconciliation between modern scientific thought and ortho-dox Christianity, it is still necessary to register the dissatisfac-tion that Torrance's emphasis on the prevenience and priority of God's grace does not do justice to the human pole of the relationship. In the quotation cited, for example, it is difficult to understand how the knower can 'yet remain free' if her full powers of rationality are not involved.

Foundationalism

This impasse is recognized by Ronald Thiemann in *Revelation and Theology*[10] and criticized by him as epistemological foundationalism. He defines foundationalism as the belief that 'knowledge' is grounded in a set of self-evident beliefs which must be established before the structure of the rest of the argument just as the first row of bricks must be laid before the rest of the building. (Non-foundationalism, on the other hand, is more adequately expressed in the imagery of woven cloth in which no one thread provides the foundation for the whole thing but in which the damage or removal of any thread can lead to the destruction of the whole thing.)

The foundationalism of classical theism lay in the belief that God was the causal foundation of creation, transcendent in his spatial and temporal detachment from created reality. Torrance's work is an attempt to redefine spatial categories in the light of Einsteinian physics. He thus avoids that foundationalism but tends towards another form of it in his emphasis on the epistemological inversion which categorizes theological knowing.

> We cannot coerce God . . . we are never allowed to impose ourselves with our notions upon Him. Knowledge of Him arises and increases out of obedient conformity to Him and the way He takes with us in revealing Himself to us . . . In theology we are concerned with statements that are pronounced primarily by God and only pronounced after Him by human subjects as hearers of His Word.[11]

However, as Thiemann points out, such an 'epistemological inversion' makes it difficult to understand how it is possible to speak about human beings having any knowledge of God because the word 'knowledge' is not being used in the sense that it is generally used in the human community.

Indeed, there is a basic contradiction inherent in Torrance's argument: revelation cannot both be rational in accordance with the terms of normal human rationality and yet utterly unique.

Torrance shows that in modern science understanding emerges from a reciprocal interaction between object and subject. The subject cannot predetermine the nature of the object but for the object to be understood it must, at least to some extent, conform with an extant conceptual scheme. This reciprocity exists even if the object is animate and yet Torrance, in his very attempt to assert the personal nature of the living God, argues that God cannot be known in that way. 'Natural objects, as we have seen, have to be objects of our cognition when we know them but it is only out of pure Grace that God gives Himself to be the object of our knowing and thinking.'[12] This does not only seem contradictory within the logic of Torrance's own attempt to argue the rationality of revelation but, ironically, makes the gracious living God less personal than inanimate objects, recalling Hartshorne's argument against the epistemological inversion of classical theism on the grounds that it implies a deficiency in God rather than his perfection.

The impasse that we find ourselves in is such that to talk about understanding God in terms of ordinary human rationality not 'as an exception to all metaphysical principles' is to treat him simply as another created object. On the other hand, if any kind of 'epistemological inversion' is asserted, then it is impossible to say how we know God. As Thiemann stringently remarks, 'The former option denies God his divinity; the latter denies us our humanity.'[13]

Non-foundationalism and narrative

His suggestion for moving beyond this impasse is to develop a non-foundational descriptive theology with 'the promises of God' as its interpretative key. Descriptive theology does not posit one universal, justificatory argument (such as God as the ultimate Cause or the universality of religious experience) but is rather a critical, reflective activity from within the Christian community and its particular conceptual framework.

> Theology (of this kind) seeks to discern the internal logic of Christian belief, i.e. it seeks to uncover the patterns of coherent interrelationships which characterise the beliefs and practices of that complex phenomenon we call the Christian faith. Theology thus presupposes that faith and

seeks through critical reflection to understand that faith more fully. Nonfoundational or descriptive theology is in this sense 'faith seeking understanding'.[14]

This is not simply subjectivism because, as has been argued earlier in this chapter, such understanding involves disciplined respect for the objectivity of that which is other than the subject. It is rather a refinement of earlier arguments that just as a marriage is not justified by one specific cause but a coinherent interplay of reasons, nevertheless it has its own appropriate logic and rightness which can be justified to, and discerned by, others outside the relationship. So the Christian faith cannot be justified by one particular foundation for that would be to tame and destroy its depth and mystery.

The most appropriate conceptual framework for Christian theology is thus not a systematic theology which depends upon a particular foundation but that of realistic narrative which provides a coherent organizing image which can take account of temporal sequence but, perhaps even more importantly, it places the emphasis on the characterization of persons in relationship with one another and responding to contingent circumstances. Narrative affirms the contingent nature of reality and the uniqueness of each person while simultaneously recognizing the interdependence of all persons. The specific Christian narrative also affirms the free will of human beings and their independence from God while making possible language about God's freedom-to-act and initiative-taking.

The category of promise

Thiemann completes his argument by suggesting that the idea of promise enables us to move beyond the methodological impasse of how it is possible to speak about the human knowing of the transcendent God for this makes possible language about the prevenient initiative of God while also allowing for a human response to those promises which can engage the full capacities of a human person.

A promise is an intentional speech-act by which the speaker assumes an obligation to perform some specified future act on behalf of the hearer. Such a speech-act, made in accord with the conventions of promising, announces the speaker's stance of commitment and obligation and describes the future act with appropriate specificity. In addition, the speaker must exhibit the requisite sincerity so that the speaker's intention to fulfil his/her obligation is communicated to the hearer in such a way that both speaker and hearer recognise that the specified future act would not come about 'in the ordinary course of events', i.e. without the speaker's intentional action.[15]

Promise is a relational category which implies both a speaker and a hearer although primacy is always granted to the one who makes the promise. It is the promiser who defines the future act, expresses the intention to perform that act, commits himself to the obligation imposed by the promise, exhibits the trustworthiness which points to its future fulfilment and who, alone, performs the act which will fulfil the promise. The one who hears the promise, on the other hand, although she is fully engaged in this reciprocal relationship cannot coerce the promiser to fulfil his obligation. For it to remain a promise, its fulfilment must depend upon the act of the promiser alone. 'To understand God's relationship to humanity under the rubric of promise is thereby to understand that relation as one in which God alone is the gracious initiator, actor and fulfiller of his own promises, i.e. to understand God as prevenient.'[16]

The response of the human person to God's promises is alays free: there is no coercion either to believe in or reject the promise. However, that response does not, in itself, effect the fulfilment or otherwise of that promise which lies in the intention and activity of God alone. For instance, as will be argued later, the resurrection of Jesus happened prior to the recognition of it by Mary Magdalene and his disciples. It did not happen as a reward for their faith or actions but purely through the freedom and grace of God. However, that is not to deny that its effectiveness was, at least partially, dependent upon their recognition and affirmation. So, the prevenience of God's gracious and loving activity is maintained at one level while simultaneously recognizing that God is involved in a relationship which makes him dependent upon human persons. The logic of promise implies free and mutual relationship while demanding that unconditional priority be given to the one who promises. God's promise is not conditional upon our merits but offers the forgiveness of sins and justification freely.

The response of the hearer of the promise depends on her relationship with the promiser, and her previous experience of his sincerity and trustworthiness because there can be no absolute guarantee that the promise will be fulfilled. The justifiability of trusting in the truthfulness of a promise is never actually confirmed (or disconfirmed) until the promiser actually fulfils (or fails to fulfil) that promise. Until the time of fulfilment the promisee must justify trust on the basis of a judgment concerning the character of the promiser.

The major difference between human partners pledging themselves to a particular action and God's promises is that the Christian believes that God is utterly trustworthy and will not fail to keep his word. Of course, that declaration of belief is itself part of the response of faith, trust and hope which arises from within a relationship with God. An atheist would not make the same declaration nor is there any self-evident proof to justify such a claim. However, within a relationship of faith such affirmation is possible although such does not mean that the believer is simply a passive recipient (as was so in classical theism and tended towards in Torrance).

This picture of the human believer engaging herself in a relationship by which she decides on the truthfulness of the nature and promises of God (as revealed in Jesus Christ and through the witness of the Bible and tradition) does not, in any way, deny the possibility of that believer exercising all her powers of thought including doubt and suspicion. In any case, as has been previously argued, the engagement of full rationality will include elements such as trust and commitment and it is those responses which will be the most appropriate for the appreciation of God's own commitment.

This picture in which both questioning and implicit belief are appropriate does offer the possibility of moving beyond our methodological impasse; it simultaneously affirms the prevenience of God while not denying the full capacity of human persons engaged in a relationship in which they change and grow, maybe sometimes moving from belief to unbelief and then returning with a new understanding and appreciation of the love in which they share. This rubric of promise implies, by definition, awareness of the openness of the future and is therefore consonant with the contention that knowledge is a process of 'becoming'.

In conclusion, our definition of the dialectical–dialogical mode of being which is love has been clarified and refined in the case of humans and God to that of the relationship between promiser and promisee, a relationship which does not deny the mutuality of the relationship while at the same time, enabling priority to be placed on God's actions. Further, since realistic narrative has been suggested as the most appropriate conceptual framework, the encounter between God and humans is best told as a love story.

4

'I Will Be Your God':

The Bible as Love Story

In the previous chapter general epistemological questions were discussed in order to examine how it is possible to speak of human beings knowing the transcendent God. In this chapter, the epistemological questions will be focussed on the identity of God asking the questions, 'Who is he?' and 'What is he like?' In order to explore these questions, two interrelated methods of philosophical analysis of personal identity will be employed: intention-action description and self-manifestation description.

The first analysis attempts to answer the question, 'What is a person like?' According to this theory, a person's identity *is* (rather than is simply indicated by) the intentions which she carried into action. Actions are thus described as enacted intentions and intentions as implicit actions. A person's identity is therefore a description of characteristic intention-action patterns across a chronological sequence. The temporal element means that the best way to answer the question, 'What is she like?' is to tell the story of her life.

This story would disclose the person's actions and her intention or will which determines those actions but it would also tell the particular circumstances and relationships to which she was responding and by which she was affected. In other words, a person is not an a-social independent entity nor can the question, 'What is she like?' be answered only in terms of self awareness for each person becomes who is she is through the interaction between her own actions and intentions to, and initiating developments in, that particular train of cicumstances which shapes her life story.

In *The Identity of Jesus Christ*,[1] Hans Frei used this methodology to ask the question, 'What was Jesus of Nazareth like' and answered by telling the life of Jesus focussing on his actions and the intentions which he displayed in behaving as he did. The fact that we did not have any account of the 'self-awareness' of Jesus is not problematical because this methodology maintains that Jesus, in common with all human beings, was not an a-social being but was what he became in relationship with others who observed him as external to themselves although they shared his life and, in that sense, knew him well.

His self was not his intention alone nor his actions alone nor was it purely his inner self-awareness nor external circumstances but a subtle interweaving of all of these over a period of time. I intend to extend Frei's approach and apply it to the narrative account of God's actions and intentions in the biblical story, arguing that this sequential narrative discloses what God is like. The fact that it is not possible to enter into God's self-awareness does not pose a problem, for if God is truly in relationship with humanity and involved in history his identity (what he is like) cannot be detached from these.

The second kind of identity analysis (self-manifestation description) attempts to answer the question, 'Who is this person?' Although the two types of analysis are ultimately inseparable this is not as easy to define as the first and is perhaps best understood by contrasting them: whereas intention-action language points towards a series of events over a period of time, self-manifestation language points to the continuity of a person's identity throughout the changing circumstances of her life. This analysis does not so much answer the question 'What is he like' but 'Who is this unique person?'

Of course, because any person is 'becoming' there will

always be an unfinished, elusive quality to such a description. Nevertheless, each self is a recognizable continuum through-out this developing personhood and changing situations, and it is this persistent selfhood which identifies this one person and no other which self-manifestation language indicates. In our discussion this methodology will be applied to both God and Jesus.

The Old Testament Convenant

Ronald Thiemann also made use of intention-action description in his suggestion of defining God as the prevenient God of promise. This was adopted in the previous chapter as a way of speaking about the relationship between the transcendent God and free, responsible human beings. The promises of God can certainly be taken as an interpretative key for the interpretation of the Bible but in this section we ask the specific questions, 'What does God promise?' and 'What does that tell us about his identity and his relationship with creation?'

What is God like?

'I will be your God and you shall be my people' sounds like a refrain throughout the Old Testament, a declaration of the covenanted partnership of mutual rights and responsibilities which God intends as the relationship between himself and Israel. The word used for covenant ('berith') does not, in itself, imply marriage but many of the Old Testament writers, especially the prophets, refined the understanding to precisely that of the nuptial covenant in which the partners do not only respect one another's distinctiveness but positively delight in it, a delight which overflows and issues in the desire that the two should become profoundly united. God does not wish that his history and creation's should henceforth be separate but that they should become one as in marriage lovers become 'no longer two but one'. It is that desire which, according to Karl Barth, the biblical Song of Songs expresses magnificently and not only justifies its inclusion in the canon but actually offers an interpretative key to the Old Testament.

> The Song of Songs is one long description of the rapture, the unquenchable yearning and the restless willingness and readiness with which both partners of this covenant hasten towards an encounter.[2]

Face-to-face covenants

In many ways it is complicated to speak about God's covenant with his creation because it is a covenant simultaneously with the whole of creation, with the human race, with the people of Israel and with each person, a complexity which is reflected in a variety of covenants mentioned in the Old Testament (e.g. Gen. 17.4, Gen. 9.12, Deut. 7.9, Jer. 31.31, Isa. 49.8). The multiplicity of these covenants do not, however, lead to contradiction because if they are seen as part of a greater whole, which this chapter aims to describe, they are all interlocking facets of the story of God's love for that which he has created, the whole picture of which does hold together in coinherent unity.

However, the covenant which God has made with the whole of creation is intensified and made explicit in the covenant which God made with humanity, that part of his creation with which he can enter into a truly loving relationship because the human capacity for rational thought and communication makes possible a dialectical/dialogical encounter.

That covenant is itself intensified in God's covenant with one nation, Israel, and even more than that with specific individuals. These covenants are not alternatives to God's universal covenant with creation: they are a re-affirmation of that covenant which in their intensity indicates the intended order and rationality of creation.

> Consider what was promised to Abraham. He was promised a place which would be *his* place, a significant role in the fruitfulness of the created time process, and the confronting presence of his God to give and determine the meaning

of his life. This is not a special privilege. It is the paradigm
of what God gives to every creature he creates – a footing
in space-time with and in the face of his own confronting
and sustaining presence.[3]

The story of Israel's dealings with God is the story of
clearly definable specific persons such as Abraham, Moses,
Hannah or Jeroboam. This is not to say that there are no
mythological overtones to stories such as Moses, nor to
advocate a literal interpretation of the text: it is simply to
affirm that these are unsubstitutable persons who cannot be
classified as 'types' or 'figures' because, although they share
characteristics with the rest of the human species, they are
who they are through the particular circumstances of their
own unrepeatable life histories. In this the Old Testament
narrative realism reflects the nature of contingent reality in
which persons 'become' not only through different circumstances but in constant relationship with other individuals
who in the uniqueness of their own life history are objective
to one another.

The uniqueness of each human being was sometimes
expressed in the Old Testament by mention of his unique
face (Gen. 48.11) and the order of contingent reality may thus
be characterized as an ever-evolving web of face-to-face
encounters. The Old Testament also witnesses to the belief
that just as individuals, each with their own face, encounter
one another so each human person can enter into such a
particular, intimate relationship with God.

There is a tension of witness here because there is on the
one hand the definite prohibition against believing that it is
possible to see the face of the transcendent God. Even Moses
on Sinai was allowed only to see the back of God 'but my face
shall not be seen' (Ex. 33.23). On the other hand, there are
several accounts of people sharing 'face-to-face' with God
(e.g. Gen. 32.30; Ex. 33.11; Deut. 34.10). However, since none
of these accounts claim that the physical lineaments of a face
were seen it appears that the phrase 'face-to-face' used here
denotes the degree of intimacy with God and the intensity of

the experience of his presence. There is thus no contradiction against the impossibility of seeing the face of the transcendent God and its corollary of prohibition against graven images.

In this light the protological myth of Adam and Eve may be interpreted as a paradigm of the whole created order, for they are created and endowed with a distinctiveness which is not intended to cause opposition nor even static juxta-position: as marriage partners they actively encounter each other in a dynamic exchange of their selves. Indeed, Adam is not deemed to be complete until he has a partner with whom he can engage in a dialectical-dialogical relationship; the animals and inanimate creation do not provide him with a possibility of such an exchange and until Eve is created he is still considered to be alone ('Then the Lord God said, "It is not good that the man should be alone. I will make him a helper fit for him"' Gen. 3.18). The face-to-face relationship of this husband and wife is normative then for interpreting the proper order of creation, but the Old Testament covenant reveals that it is also normative as a definition for the engagement between the Creator and that which he has made, 'for your Maker is your husband' (Isa. 54.5).

The law of love

The Genesis myth also expresses the reason why God's intention of partnership with humanity has not been fulfilled. It is not so much that the cause of sin is explained in the myth but that its nature and effects are defined: sin is defined as disobedience to God's will and its effect is the fracturing of the respectful and loving exchange between God and humans and humans and each other.

That such a commandment and demand for obedience is made by God followed up by such a punishment may well be seen to give credence to that picture of God which the first chapter recognized as contributing to the decline of religious belief: the picture of a capricious tyrant who is jealous of his own power and knowledge and who can hardly be conceived of as a 'God of Love'.

In order to answer such an interpretation, the question

needs to be asked, 'What is the will of God which Adam and Eve disobeyed?' The answer, partly implied in the myth itself, is expanded throughout the Old Testament writing's dual emphasis on the true worship and social justice. The Mosaic Torah makes clear that God's will is that humans should live together in a responsible and mutually compassionate community in which the things which are prohibited are those things which offend against the objective dignity and rights of others, thereby degrading them (e.g. Ten Commandments: Ex. 20).

In the Old Testament (specially the prophetic canon) it is also made clear that the responsible ordering of the economic, political, and cultural aspects of the human community is inextricably linked with the worship of the true God. This is not simply a question of giving complementary respect to God and others. Truly to love God involves love of the neighbour, for each person is in covenant with God: to abuse another person is to hurt God because the one who is being abused is God's beloved covenant partner. It is not possible to enter into a truly loving relationship (one in which there is a mutual addressing) with God while at the same time degrading, abusing or manipulating a fellow human being, because that is not to recognize the identity and will of God with whom one claims to be in relationship. It is as much a denial of God's true self to live irresponsibly in relation to other people as it is to worship pagan idols.

The presence of God

The defining phenomenology of love suggested that in love, a person comes to participate in the life of the beloved. To love God, then, is to come to share in his life which is eternal. Hence, the testimony (again expressed in the Genesis myth) that death is the result of sin. However, it should be interpreted in this light of self-infliction through the refusal to love fully rather than as a cruel punishment of a tyrannical God: by refusing to love the true God human beings condemn themselves to live only mortal life which necessarily ends in death rather than in sharing the eternal life of God.

Similarly, there are accounts of people who have come to share profoundly in the life of God. The very writings of the Old Testament themselves are testimony to the fact that there were people who turned to God and addressed him in worship: in petition, praise, confession and indeed in lamentation, questioning and anger as they participate in the intimacy and honesty of a love relationship.

Where these people have exerted their influence by testifying to God and working for justice and righteousness, the language of intimacy and participation is used about them and God. God is even said to dwell in the reality he has created, not only in the temple where he is addressed in worship and ritual but also in the human heart which is humble enough to acknowledge creaturely dependency and confess the sin which has prevented full loving (Isa. 57.15).

The presence of God, that deep union between himself and creation, is also expressed in language about the spirit of God. Although this is not worked out in any systematic exposition such language is a consistent affirmation of people sharing in the life of God through rightful worship and the establishment of the responsible society (Isa. 42 and 61).

Yet, for all the Old Testament witness (which must not be underestimated or dismissed as unloving legalism), it is certainly true that any real union between God and humans with all which that involves is only partial and feebly established. The fulfilment of God's hopes for the establishment of the order of love (which since this means the establishment of the sovereignty of the will of God is sometimes spoken of as God's kingdom) still lies in the future and his intention is still essentially promises for the *eschaton*.

However, God does not wait passively for humans to act in obedience to his will: he actively works for that, encouraging his people and hoping that as he turned to them in love so they will come to turn to him. It is as if he is wooing his beloved, taking the initiative to declare and offer his love but out of respect for her freedom of decision he can only wait upon her response. Yet both the longed-for future of mutual relationship and his present wooing are signs of his love for her and are, therefore, both spoken of in the language of intimate participation and the indwelling of God's spiritual presence with his people (e.g. Joel 2.28–32 and Ezek. 37 as a sign of future consummation and Micah 3.8 as a sign of the active present involvement of God).

God's words in the law and prophetic preaching have indicated his intention. His promises have done likewise and these have been ratified by his steadfast faithfulness in the face of varying responses from his beloved (both individuals and the nation of Israel), for this is no closed *egoisme à deux*: Israel's life is concerned with many other matters and relationships in economic, political, military and territorial spheres. These contingent concerns and events, over which God had no autocratic control, were such important aspects of the life of Israel in which he longed to share that they could not be irrelevant to him or their relationship.

So, although he always respected the contingency of these events and Israel's response to them, he continually addressed her in the face of them, hoping to persuade her that it is only by turning to him in love that her full selfhood which he can discern and longs to call forth, will be fulfilled in the mutual sharing of their lives. Whatever happens and whatever her response, however, God declares that he will always be faithful to her.

Israel as unfaithful wife

God is determined that 'I will be your God and you shall be my people'. There is, nevertheless, one overwhelming obstacle to that mutuality which is that expressed in the protological myth: human sinfulness. Throughout the Old Testament God reveals himself as the pure and holy God. It is a holiness revealed both in terms of transcendence, especially on Mount Sinai but also in terms of social justice and righteousness (e.g. Amos 5.21–24; Isa. 58.6–9). This holiness is his objective identity which cannot be compromised. It is his face which humans must recognize if they are to engage in this partnership.

It is sin which separates humans from God and which must be overcome before humans can enter into any meaningful encounter with God. However, God does not only make this as a demand, he also actively encourages and enables his beloved to refrain from sinning: the religious cult (especially the various rituals of atonement) as well as the laws and prophetic witness are all part of the invitation and assistance in which God offers a way by which the sin which separates them may be overcome and their partnership consummated. Then the covenant can be truly made between God and each person in their heart (Jer. 31.31–34). Perhaps this is partly why the fulfilment of this promise and intention came to be identified with one particular agent of God who in various titles such as the Messiah, the Christ, the Son of God, Son of Man, the Suffering Servant was conceived of as one who lives in obedience to God, restores Israel's fortunes and contributes to the establishment of God's kingdom.

The gulf between God and humanity created by sin cannot be overemphasized: it is a fundamental characteristic of their relationship. Again, the protological myth communicates the fact that it is not 'encounter' which characterizes relationships within creation, but broken partnerships.

Thus the quotation from Karl Barth is only partially true: it is not encounter nor even passionate yearning and wooing which characterize the love story of God and Israel or each human person. It is the fact that this relationship has previously been marred and broken by the human partner who persists in living sinfully.

There is a history to this relationship: they are not two new lovers who have recently met and who court on that basis, but partners whose relationship has been damaged and fractured by the refusal of one partner to turn to the other but which God continually endeavours to restore. On that understanding, it is not the Song of Songs but the prophetic book of Hosea which can be seen as the interpretative key of the Old Testament.

Who is God?

As far as the other type analysis (the self-manifestation description) is concerned, the question 'Who is God?' can be answered in the following ways.

Firstly, the narrative sequence of the Old Testament defines God as the transcendent Creator: this may sound like tautology but it is intended to establish that the God whom the Old Testament identifies is the true God, the transcendent source of life and not a mere idol.

However, God does not only create: he also continues to be involved with, and takes responsibility for, that which he creates, accepting the implications of the relationship into which he has entered. This may be seen as a corollary to the definition of God as Promiser because he accepts the responsibility of being obedient to the promises which he has made to his creatures and actively works to establish the covenant which he intends.

Since he is perfectly holy, he cannot consort with sin and he makes that abundantly clear to his loved one but he also accepts responsibility for this problem in the relationship and offers ways in which atonement can be effected and sin overcome.

Of course, to affirm that God takes responsibility does not deny that he continues to respect the freedom and integrity of his beloved but, whatever happens and in spite of the hurt which he feels because of her continuing faithlessness, he is always completely faithful and forgiving. He takes the initiative to restore the estranged relationship, offering his love freely and graciously. God is thus not only Creator but also Redeemer.

The God of the Old Testament has often been depicted as an angry God, the message retributive and the need for atonement legalistic. It has thus been contrasted to the New Testament, which has been seen as the covenant of love. In fact, the Old Testament story also narrates that God is Love. This is more than saying that God loves or is loving. The very identity of God is love, in all circumstances he responds lovingly and in this he is always true to himself. He cannot do otherwise.

However, this perfect self-relatedness, as has already been defined, is a self-relatedness of utter selflessness in which he can only find his fulfilment and be true to his identity by turning to his beloved. Such selflessness is, indeed, the reason why the story can be told at all, for it is only the fact that in this selflessness the transcendent God has accommodated himself to human thought forms that has made possible the dialogue which is the basis of the Old Testament narrative. That narrative defines God in terms of the definition of love which has developed throughout this story (i.e. dialectical, dialogical, overflowing, participatory, committed, vulnerable, particular, involving knowledge and yet mysterious). More particularly, it defines God as one who forgives and who takes responsibility and initiative.

In the light of this interpretation, there is no contradiction between the Old and New Testament: they are part of a whole story in which God is seen as Creator and Redeemer.

The Life of Jesus Christ

That love story reached new intensity in the life of Jesus Christ to which we now turn, and to which the same two identity analyses will be applied.

What was Jesus like?

If the intention-action analysis of selfhood is applied to the life of Jesus as told in the four Gospels one particular motif becomes discernible as characteristic of his life: obedience.

His obedience

His obedience is, in fact, emphasized more than other qualities which might have seemed more likely to be mentioned such as his faith or love. It must be defined more exactly as his obedience to God i.e. Jesus is the man who purposefully enacts his own intentions in conformity with the intentions of God.

His obedience to the will of God is discerned in the Gospel

accounts of his ministry in which the preaching, healing and miracles are recognized as the establishment of God's eschatological kingdom. The person of Jesus is inextricably linked with the kingdom: he both proclaimed and lived a life in which he loved (i.e. respected and delighted in) God and his fellow human beings. In other words, he fulfilled the Old Testament law in loving both God and all persons (Luke 22.37–40), and the fulfilment of God's promise of covenanted love was discerned to be already happening in Jesus.

He was recognized to be in constant relationship with God, referring all things to him and acknowledging his dependency on him. It was this which led others to identify him as 'sent from God', one with a mission to be obedient to God's will. That which prevented growth into a full selfhood of persons within a caring, responsible community was believed to have been overcome in Jesus and he was identified as being 'without sin'. Traditional commentators would probably interpret this to mean that he never sinned, whereas modern interpreters (placing great emphasis on Heb. 5.8) would argue that he *became* sinless and *learned* obedience. Since intention-action analysis assumes that a person becomes over a period of time, such a variety in interpretation is not problematical and all that needs to be acknowledged is that other people recognized Jesus as 'sinless', perfectly loving God and others.

Both the sinlessness of Jesus and his mission and identification with the kingdom are focussed together in the story of his baptism, one of the clearest intention-action patterns of the Synoptic Gospels (Matt. 3.13–15).

In asking to be baptized, although others queried his need for repentance, he was clearly intending to identify himself with the rituals of purification and atonement proscribed in the Old Testament. His physical action thus reveals his intention to be obedient to the will of God 'to fulfil all righteousness'.

The obedience of Jesus to God is also characteristic of the passion narratives and in these the unique personal identity of Jesus is defined particularly clearly in the consistent intention-action pattern of the story: Jesus intends to do his Father's will and his actions are determined by that as he 'set his face to go to Jerusalem' (Luke 9.51). That pattern is perhaps most obviously delineated in Gethsemane when he explicitly utters the words which others have recognized as definitive of his life, 'Yet not what I will, but what Thou wilt.'

His vocation

It is inevitable that the two phases of Jesus' life, in Galilee and Jerusalem, should be seen separately because, to a certain extent, that is how the Gospel writers present them. However, the distinction between them can be over-emphasized and a false dichotomy made. In order to do justice to the continuity of his personal identity, the early ministry of Jesus should not just be seen as a preliminary which he left behind as he moved on to Jerusalem, nor should his arrest and death be considered as simply the unfortunate consequence of his words and actions. Somehow a dialectic must be maintained between the life-affirming ministry of Jesus and his willingness to die the death of a sinless victim.

That dialectic and a key to what 'Jesus was like' lies in that which he proclaimed and lived in his Galilee ministry: the conviction that he was working in accordance to the will of God in whom he delighted, and that his message was to proclaim that God's kingdom was beginning to be established through the gracious initiative of God. In that kingdom, all that prevents full selfhood will be overcome in healing power and reconciling love. God's covenant promises are beginning to be fulfilled in this man's life which overflows with delight in, and respect for, others and, above all, with delight and trust in God in relationship with whom his very identity is rooted. The ministry of Jesus so burgeons with an abundance of life that it would be inappropriate to do anything else but rejoice in it. The Bridegroom's presence makes celebration inevitable (Mark 2.19).

This rejoicing, however, is not indulgent hedonism, for the ministry of Jesus is characterized also by his identification with those whose lives were anything but fulfilled abundantly (Mark 2.17). It is not possible, nor necessary, to tell the whole Gospel story at this juncture nor to analyse why Jesus precipitated opposition but the point is simply made here that his death and passion were already interwoven into his Galilee ministry and not merely sequential to it.

> The thrust of his whole life is towards his death as something desired, chosen, embraced in love out of a fulness of humanity. It is remembered ... as freely chosen identification in compassion with the deepest human anguish. It is a choice of victimhood, of the worst, of the unthinkable, a self-determined immersion in the tortuous and tortured ambiguities of created life.[4]

This act of love is important because otherwise the passion of Jesus might be seen as a form of masochism or stoic obedience in the face of disaster, rather than as a vocation lived in the same attitude as he lived out his earlier vocational ministry; believing in the gracious initiative of the God who was other than himself and in whom he delighted and trusted as Creator and Redeemer. *All* the ministry of Jesus in Galilee and Jerusalem was characterized by this sense of God's pervading presence in his life.

The presence of the absent God

That having been said, it must immediately be countered by saying that all the ministry of Jesus was also characterized by the absence of God, for as Dietrich Bonhoeffer and others have remarked, the God of the Gospel passion narratives is the 'absent' God who does not come to rescue Jesus. 'The God who is with us is the God who forsakes us (Mark 15.34). The God who lets us live in the world without the working hypothesis of God is the God before whom we stand continually. Before God and with God we live without God.'[5]

Jesus lived his life (in both Galilee and Jerusalem) in

obedience to the law of love, responsibly, compassionately, and to the point of his own vulnerability. He did so because he could do no other if he was to be true to himself and he did so, as Bonhoeffer commented, *etsi deus non daretur* – even if there was no God. 'God himself compels us to recognize it. So our coming of age leads us to a true recognition of our situation before God. God would have us know that we must live as men who manage our lives without him.'

The humanity of Jesus, then, is an important focus of attention and a potential starting point for any discussion of the Christian faith, another key element in the coherent interplay of non-foundational key elements. This focus on the human subject is not primarily a result of the modern philosophical movements charted in the opening chapter but, as Bonhoeffer recognized, the truth demanded by an honest reading of the Gospel accounts of the life of Jesus. It is not cnly his relationship with God and his talk of God which is important but what he is as a man in himself, including the elements of his humanity such as fear or even apparent lovelessness which have traditionally tended to be ignored as incompatible with the perfect Son of God. So, for example, Rosemary Haughton's interpretation of his apparent rudeness to Mary at the wedding at Cana as the perfectly normal separation of child from mother asks serious questions about the definition of sinlessness.[6]

This then is the dialectic which must be maintained in speaking about Jesus: his life was characterized by the constant presence of the transcendent God in relationship with whom his very identity is located, and yet he lived responsibly as a self-determining man in the ambiguity of contingent created reality *etsi deus non daretur*.

The question 'What was Jesus like?' may be answered by telling the story of his life: his identification with the kingdom of God as presently and graciously realized, his obedience to the call of God, his intention to live in accordance with God's will and his consequent vulnerability matched and overmatched by his trust in the presence of the 'absent' God.

Who is Jesus Christ?

The problem of continuing this discussion with the question, 'Who is Jesus?' at this point is that to do so tends to give the impression that a neat linear progression of argument was made by the first Christians and can be made still, i.e. the argument would run that God revealed himself in the Old Testament. Jesus of Nazareth was seen to be in conformity with God, then the resurrection showed that Jesus was divine. Apart from avoiding many serious questions, such a linear analysis does not do justice to the complexity of how the disciples came to understand who Jesus was.

The Gospel accounts of the life of Jesus were themselves kerygmatic, written in response to the resurrection. In the same way, it might well be argued that the interpretation which this study has placed on the Old Testament God as Love can only be made in the light of the belief that Jesus of Nazareth further identified God. The point must be made that the story cannot be told in a simple chronological sequence without acknowledging the complexity of how people did actually come to answer the question, 'Who is Jesus?' However, there must also be some linear element in order to do justice to the temporal reality of the early church: a narrative account grounds in history the momentum of 'faith seeking understanding' which the first Christians followed.

The agent of God's love

The identification of Jesus with the kingdom, his sinlessness and explicit association with the ritual of atonement led others to identify him in terms of the various Old Testament prophecies of redemption (e.g. Isa. 11.1, Micah 4) and promises of a particular agent of God's redeeming love and eschatological restoration of his intention for creation. He was thereby identified as a man in union with God and thus the language of participation an indwelling of God's spirit which was noted in the Old Testament is intensified in the description of Jesus (e.g. Luke 13.21, Matt. 12.28, Mark 1.10, Luke 4.18, John 3.34).

In the passion and crucifixion that identification became refined into equating Jesus with the various agents of ritual sacrificial atonement such as the scapegoat, Passover Lamb, Suffering Servant (Isa. 53) or the Christ for whom it was necessary that 'he should suffer these things and enter into his glory' (Luke 24.26).

In view of the fact that the whole story of a person's life must be told before self-manifestation language may be properly applied, the resurrection, the 'end' of this particular life story must be taken into account and the question asked, 'What does the resurrection say about who Jesus is?'

At the very least, the resurrection was taken as a confirmation of God's approval of Jesus of Nazareth. God has thus acted decisively to identify himself with this particular man as only the transcendent God can: he created life, raising a man from the dead in a second 'creation out of nothing'. Jesus thus comes to share in the life of the immortal, eternal God.

Here it is important to use the language of 'glorification' and 'exaltation' in reference to the risen Jesus because the Gospel narratives indicate that he was not merely resuscitated but moved to a different sphere of existence from that of human historical experience. In order for a human person to be sharing in the glorified life of God, sin must have been overcome. God had promised that such redemption would be effected in the Messiah or the Christ and even more specifically in the suffering of the Lamb of God or Servant of God. The resurrection thus confirms the identification of Jesus as the agent of God's redeeming love.

God incarnate

However, this interpretation does not do justice to the New Testament witness, and its adoptionism is inadequate in terms of later Christological reflection, for although the New Testament is far from arguing that there is any ontological unity between Jesus and God, it does point towards the ascription of divinity to Jesus Christ which later became explicitly formulated in the credal statements of Chalcedon and Nicaea. It is not so much that the titles 'Lord' or 'Son of God' are used of him, because neither of these words is an unambiguous acknowledgment of divinity.

There are, however, other indications that Jesus Christ came to be regarded as more than a human agent of God: Thomas identifies him as 'my Lord and my God', he is worshipped (Matt. 28.9 and 11) and in the more sophisticated conceptual developments of Col. 1.15–17 and the Johannine prologue (John 1.1–17) he is seen as pre-existent.

If it is not accurate to say that the risen Jesus was simply equated with God, it is also not accurate to suggest that the later creeds and definitions of Jesus Christ as 'fully divine' and 'fully human' were accretions to, and aberrations from, the original experience of those who encountered Jesus risen from the dead. According to these credal conceptualizations the question 'Who is Jesus?' is answered by saying not only 'He is the human agent of God's redemption' but also 'He is God incarnate.'

The subtle intricacies of the debate of 'the myth of God incarnate' are too complex to examine in this brief discussion.[7] There is thus no intention in this work of asking the question 'Did God become incarnate in Jesus of Nazareth?' but rather to pursue a far more modest aim of asking 'Is it possible that God could have become incarnate in Jesus?' This question itself might helpfully be sub-divided into 'Is Jesus of Nazareth "in character" with the story of the identity of God to such an extent that he could have been recognized as God incarnate?' and secondly, 'Is it possible for God to become incarnate?'

Is Jesus like God?

This question has already been explored in the examination of the obedience of Jesus to God: as Jesus is the one who lived in conformity to the will of God this question is answered in the affirmative. The Old Testament narrates that God is selfless even to the point of vulnerable dependency. Self-limitation is thus a consistent characteristic of God's narrated self-manifestation and the 'self-limitation' of incarnation would therefore be 'in character'.

Indeed, the fact that humans are able to say anything at all about the transcendent God implies that he has limited himself to becoming involved in temporal history and accessible to human concepts and categories of understanding.

Furthermore, the complex narrative structure of the biblical text refines this idea of God's self-limitation. In the Hebrew scripture God is the 'main character' and yet his direct actions are only rarely described. Most often God's activity is depicted through the description of others' activity. In order to make this point, Thiemann uses the example of the two versions of the election of King David. In the first version (I Sam. 16) the election is described as the direct result of God's intervention. In the second (beginning at I Sam. 17) accounts of human decision and action predominate and God remains a silent force in the background, yet decisive in that the conclusion is still made that the election has been intended by God. Both strands of narrative are needed to depict the identity of God: the transcendent God who is involved in, and takes responsibility for, his creation and yet does so in such a way that he allows human beings to be free agents.[8]

This complexity of narration reaches its zenith in the life of Jesus. In the opening of the Synoptic Gospels, Jesus is identified with the kingdom of God and thus, by implication, with the Old Testament's Covenant, will, promises and commandments of God. This point is made particularly clearly in Matthew and Luke in which the birth narratives define him in a somewhat stylized fashion as the fulfiller of the Old Testament promises but it is made in all three Synoptic Gospels in the way in which God's direct intervention and involvement is emphasized in the earlier part of the ministry: there the miracles happen and, most significantly, the only examples of direct speech by God are at the baptism and transfiguration.

As the story progresses in the ministry at Jerusalem, Jesus becomes less stylized and more clearly defined as a unique historical person. God's direct involvement becomes noticeably absent, as has been previously noted, in the passion narrative: he does not come to rescue Jesus in answer to his pleas in Gethsemane nor does he save him from the cross (Matt. 27.43). Even in the account of the resurrection when the power of God is at its height (for only the transcendent God can actually create life 'out of nothing') there is no direct mention of God as active agent.

Yet the narrative makes clear that Jesus is acting as he does because he believes himself to be directed by God and in conformity to his will. (Mark 14.36, Luke 24.26, Matt. 17.22). Jesus trusts in God's promises, which as promises, by definition, cannot be proved to be trustworthy until they have been fulfilled in the future. He thus walks by faith not by sight and refuses to seek for premature comfort for his own sake but rather chooses to remain obedient to God's law of love.

The complex interweaving of the Gospel narrative pattern thus argues for the self-effacing nature of God's power and presence which is involved in contingent reality and does accept responsibility for his own creation yet in such a way that he enables Jesus, whose life is full of the presence of God, to become truly himself 'even if there is no God'.

Can God become incarnate?

Of course this is still to argue the case for Jesus being recognized as the agent of God's redeeming love rather than as God incarnate. That question can only be answered from a participatory involvement in the world to which the scriptural narrative testifies. There is no one foundational truth which must be adhered to as incontrovertible proof of the incarnation, and in this non-foundational complexity the most appropriate form of theological reflection would seem to be a narrated description of the cluster of beliefs and interpretative keys to which the question 'Within that particular world-view does it "fit" that God would and could become incarnate?' may be applied.

In order to answer that question, examination must be made of what are the implications for God's identity of

94 *For Your Maker is Your Husband*

stating that he became incarnate. Belief in the incarnation implies that God took the initiative to become a sinless man in order to restore the broken relationship between himself and humanity. God's taking the initiative to forgive is consistent with the insights of the book of Hosea, earlier defined as the interpretative key of the Old Testament.

The narrative, in fact, goes further and indicates that God graciously repays betrayal with promises of an even deeper intimacy (Jer. 31.34) and since the capacity to do so is traditionally believed to be the prerogative of God alone he thus precipitates opposition. Finally, in the resurrection narratives Jesus returns to those who betrayed him and offers deeper intimacy and greater responsibility.

Within this overarching story of God's identity ranging from the Old Testament to the resurrection it 'fits' to say both that God would take the initiative to restore the broken relationship and that he would forgive. Given that story, it is not improbable that the only way for a human to be sinless is for God to take the initiative and himself become incarnate.

Another implication of belief in the incarnation is that God became incarnate in the specific historical person of Jesus of Nazareth. This unsubstitutable particularity of a man is in conformity with what has been noted about the Old Testament focus on specific historical persons. It also accords with the attitude of respect for the freedom and objectivity of the human beings to whom he gives responsibility and encourages but never overpowers or coerces. Even the complex narration of the 'presence' and 'absence' of God is in conformity with this understanding of God's respect for human beings.

None of this is to prove that the incarnation did happen and certainly not that it was inevitable, for in this, as in all things, the transcendent God is free to act as he wills constrained only by the 'necessity of love'. It does, however, answer the question of the possibility of the incarnation in the affirmative.

Christological language

The logic of this narrated description of beliefs is that the stories of the identity of both God and Jesus coalesce and reach their mutual climax in the resurrection and neither can be understood apart from the other. The life of Jesus can only be properly interpreted by placing him in the context of God's relationship with Israel. God can only be defined with reference to Jesus. Neither is the epistemological foundation but rather they reciprocally identify one another.

Indeed, there is no one foundation to this story. Even the starting point of this particular exploration – that God is Love – cannot be taken as such a foundation, for that statement is made particularly in response to the life of Jesus, whose self-relatedness was that of utter selflessness and thus of love. Not even that declaration that God is Love can be the single foundation, for all such statements exist together in co-inherent, perichoretic unity.

The truth of the reciprocal identification yet differentiation of Jesus and God explains the momentum towards the credal statements of Chalcedon and Nicaea. It became clear to the patristic theologians that in order to do justice to the significance of Jesus Christ it was necessary to employ a unitary approach in which they paid respect to him 'as he was in himself'. That is to say, they sought to give expression to his wholeness and integrity as one Person who is both God and man.

The creeds were formulated as a response to the experience of the first witnesses, and although the philosophical conceptualization may seem to be so very different from the Gospel narratives, it was an wholly appropriate and responsible endeavour to engage the human intellect in understanding the way God has acted in relation to humanity. Once again, 'neither theological concepts nor original narratives and images are foundational but a constant movement between the two ensures a mutual enrichment'.[9]

For all the difficulties involved in christological language, it is important that some conceptualization be made because, as Colin Gunton remarks, 'at stake are not simply matters of irrelevant cosmology but the ability to bring to expression the love of God ... and the freedom of the eternal to identify himself with us'.[10]

The glory of God in the face of Christ

Moreover, the epistemology of knowing and loving which has been explored can press this idea further. That epistemology spoke of the loving self being shaped by the other and sharing so profoundly in that other's life to such an extent that he participates in that other's very self, i.e. they indwell one another. Longstanding Christian tradition has spoken of human believers dwelling in God so that they become like him and even bear his image. A popular devotional book, for instance, expresses the phenomonology of love assumed in such an idea.

> Those who live together over a long time can also come to look alike because they think alike, they reflect each other. Those who live with the Lord become his mirror. His face is reflected in theirs in such a way that they become his living images, radiant with his glory (II Corinthians 3.18).[11]

Of course, bearing the features of the beloved is not literally true. It does, however, give symbolic expression to a particular characteristic of love and is in conformity with the theological reflections, mainly deriving from the insights of the Greek Fathers, which see Christian existence as a 'growing into his likeness'.[12]

This is, as has been said, a longstanding and recurrent tradition. Yet this characteristic of love has not been commonly applied to the other partner of this loving relationship, i.e. to God. If God does truly love, then he will come to participate, to 'indwell' human history and life, and can be said to be as likely to become a partaker of human nature as much as humans might become partakers of the divine nature (II Peter 1.14).

If humans can come to bear the features of God, then he can come to bear the features of a human person. This is in line with Paul's testimony, 'For it is the God who said, "Let light shine out of darkness," who has shone in our hearts to give us the light of the knowledge of the glory of God in the face of Christ' (II Cor. 4.6).

Perhaps the most profound meditation and amplification of this idea is Dante's final vision in the *Divine Comedy*, in which the full self-manifestation of the Godhead is revealed as three perichoretic circles of light in which the lineaments of a human face can be distinguished. God's very self has been shaped by his involvement with humanity.

> Eternal light, that in Thyself alone
> Dwelling, alone dost know Thyself, and smile
> On Thy self love, so knowing and so known ...
> When I had looked on it a little while –
> Seemed in itself, and in its own self hue.
> Limned with our image ...[13]

The truth which christological conceptualization and language have tried to express is that God's identity cannot be separated from the life of Jesus of Nazareth. In other words, there is no essential divinity or 'hidden God' who is different from Jesus Christ. His identity is none other than 'the face of Christ'.

The doctrine of exchange

Belief in the incarnation is consistent with the self-limitation and self-emptying (kenosis) of God which was revealed in the Old Testament covenant of love and which Paul came to articulate as the cardinal characteristic of Jesus Christ's personal identity (Phil. 2.5–8).

I would prefer to use the terminology of self-giving (rather than 'limiting' or 'emptying') because it implies a relationship rather than simply the attribute of an individual. As such it is more expressive of the biblical witness to the relationship with humans which compels God to give himself away e.g. 'For our sake he made him to be sin who knew no sin, that in him we might become the righteousness of God (II Cor. 5.21. See also II Cor. 8.9).

These Pauline verses were amplified by the later church

into an explicit formulation of the idea of exchange, God coming to share in human life that humans might come to share in his life. The idea was expressed by various writers in various ways but the formulation was always basically the same as that made by the twelfth century Cistercian, Guerric of Igny.

> O wonderful exchange . . . you take flesh and give divinity, a commerce in charity . . . emptying yourself, you have filled us. You have poured into all men all the plenitude of your divinity. You have transformed but not confounded.[14]

Jesus as human bridegroom

Before proceeding this seems to be the most appropriate point to reflect on the possibility that Jesus of Nazareth could have married. As has already been noted, throughout the history of the church there have been apocryphal legends about the marriage or love affair between Jesus and Mary Magdalene. Its historicity is of no concern here, but it is relevant for the theological questions which it raises about the incarnation.

Firstly, it raises the question of the sexuality of Jesus. Any hesitation about acknowledging the possibility of Jesus being married can probably be traced to the traditional equation between sexuality and sinfulness but if the tenets of this work are to be applied, then the willing exchange of selves in a responsible sexual relationship of mutual respect and delight is less sinful, more loving and more human than the one who in hard-heartedness, arrogance and fear detaches herself from the risk of encounter with an other.

Of course, this is not to imply that only those engaged in active sexual relationships are fully human, but simply to deny an equation between sexuality *per se* and sinfulness. Sexuality also includes sexual urges and feelings which may not be expressed overtly in a relationship but which are a fundamental constituent of human nature. If the full humanity of Jesus is to be affirmed, as credal definition states, then the possibility of Jesus experiencing sexual attraction must be acknowledged. As John Robinson remarks, the following question is 'a good one to ask yourself in order to test your reaction'.

When the woman wiped Jesus' feet she performed a highly sexual action. Did Jesus at that moment experience an erection?[15]

Secondly, the question of Mary Magdalene raises the issue of the particularity of love. A great deal has already been written about the particularity of God's relationship with Israel revealing rather than denying his love for the rest of creation. Likewise, the special love of Jesus need not have denied his love for others. This point, however, needs to be pressed further. Donald MacKinnon has argued that the church still needs to come to terms with the shattering implications of the incarnation.

What it was for him to be human was to be subject to the sort of fragmentation of effort, curtailment of design, interruption of purpose, distraction of resolve that belongs to temporal existence. To leave one place for another is to leave work undone; to give attention to one suppliant is to ignore another; to expend energy today is to leave less for tomorrow.[16]

Any talk of Jesus loving everyone equally may well be construed as our inability and unwillingness to acknowledge the degree of self-limitation which God accepted in becoming incarnate. This sentence might well be added to MacKinnon's list: 'To love one person specially and to spend time with her alone is to leave others outside the possibility of intimacy with you.' The picture of Jesus loving everyone equally, it has to be said, has more to do with a superhuman being than an ordinary man constrained by the limitations of temporal existence. To speak of Jesus marrying Mary Magdalene, however improbable that may have been historically, does take the idea of God's self-limitation to the extreme in acknowledging the limitations of the human Jesus.

Life in the Holy Spirit

The stories of the identity of Jesus and God coalesce and climax in the passion and resurrection: God's identity is now plainly revealed in the face of Jesus Christ and his intentions toward his beloved cannot be more evident. Yet that hope of covenanted love cannot be completed until the response of the human partner is included in the account of the love story.

R. C. Moberly, in his book *Atonement and Personality*[17] commented that it is difficult to comprehend the atonement simply in terms of the relationship between Jesus and God because it is impossible to see how one man's relationship with God can be said to have overcome sin and death. If, however, that relationship affected the lives of other men and women then it becomes possible to comprehend how individual lives and corporate societies can begin to be lived in accordance with the will of God and thus restore the estranged relationship. Moberly's comment is that the atonement cannot be understood with reference to Calvary alone but only in relation to Pentecost as well.

The conceptualization of the faith which can be traced in the early church followed the same momentum; the patristic theologians came to realize that christological definition by itself was not adequate but needed to be completed by the Trinitarian formula. Trinitarianism does more than simply express that difference and relationship are the nature of the Godhead, for a binary relationship between Father and Son alone would do that (as indeed Process theology's di-polar concept would).

What traditional Trinitarian logic with its 'second difference' of the Holy Spirit does is to allow the possibility of speaking about human participation in God's life in terms of co-inherence, destroying neither the identity of God nor humanity. If the only relationship 'in God' was that of Father and Son or even if the Spirit was conceived of as a bond between them, then the human believer could not participate in that relationship but only acknowledge it and perhaps imitate it.

Any language of participatory identification would suggest some sort of mystical dissolution into the person of Christ which would destroy the uniqueness of both. On the other hand, to conceive of the Spirit as separate from the Son and yet still part of the Godhead is to allow for the possibility of human participation in the atoning process without denying the uniqueness of the action of Jesus. Thus, though the human believer, in the Spirit, participates in the continuing sufferings and triumphs of the Christian life, there is no strict analogy between her life and the incarnation.

Once again, it is not possible to locate one foundational cause to explain such a momentum. Certainly, it is important that the disciples knew themselves to be forgiven and felt compelled by the resurrection to make a decision about the real identity of God. That same decision has to be faced by all witnesses: Do you recognize that Jesus defines God and therefore do you accept all the corollary implications of what that says about God and obeying his will? As a decision, by definition, it is made freely and consciously by human persons and yet the experience of encounter with God which compels that decisiveness is such that the choice is experienced as being made only in the prevenient grace of God.

In order for a person to affirm that Jesus is Lord the presence of God must already be in his life (I Cor. 12.3). So, in the Trinitarian logic, the Holy Spirit may well be the starting point for any discussion of the covenant of God and human persons.

The life of love

An examination of the identity and function of the Holy Spirit is difficult because it is about the response of each unique person and particular communities in particular circumstances. The very diversity of subjects, then, makes a short discussion very difficult. However, it seems to be important at this point to emphasize that if humans do respond to the resurrection with recognition and commitment then they have accepted the graciousness of God's love in their lives and the covenant has at last become mutual love.

All the effects of love noted in the earlier outline of love can be found in the New Testament epistles written 'in the power of the Holy Spirit'. Fundamentally, the human person is in love with God and feels that it is only in relationship with God-in-Christ that she is really her true self (Phil. 1.21, Gal. 2.20). In that love a re-definition of the self's identity is experienced, a fundamental re-orientation of one's life which the Bible defines as *metanoia* or conversion. Since the past history of this love affair has been one of misunderstanding and estrangement this 'turning to' the beloved God will issue in tears of contrition for past failures (Acts 3.19, II Cor. 7.10, Rom. 2.4). Yet, in the mutual exchange of love, that past is healed and the human partner recognizes, as if for the first time, God's past protestations of love and his intentions (Eph. 1.3–10) and is grateful not only for God's faithfulness but also for his initiative in restoring and consummating the covenant (II Cor. 5.8).

This joy of recognition issues in the dialogical sharing of love in which God's continual addressing of humanity is reciprocated in the human speech of worship (Col. 3.16), vows of commitment (John 21.15) and testimony to that love so that others may understand the reason for such re-orientation. All of this is done in the same paradoxical spirit of freedom and compulsion with which a person declares 'I love you'. Those in love with God in Christ can do no other but speak that love (I Cor. 9.16).

Love is also dialogical in the sense that each partner continually 'calls forth' the selfhood of the other. This is easy to understand in the case of the human lover who feels that 'in Christ' she is most truly herself and that what this relationship offers is indeed love (i.e. she is an I not an It). This sense of freedom and fulfilment is ever deepening in a growing relationship (Phil. 3.12). However, it is somewhat more difficult to speak about God's 'becoming' through this relationship (the precise conceptualization will be examined in the later discussion of the economic and immanent Trinity). It is not, however, impossible to conceive that as humans respond in love and openness to God they will come to feel that love as new and constantly deepening whereas, in fact, it has always been freely offered. It is not God who has changed but his human lovers (I John 2.7), but the reciprocal exchange does, at last, enable the love to deepen and grow whereas rejection and estrangement stymies its development.

This in itself indicates the need for a long term commitment to God, a marriage which is made 'for better or for worse' in the face of a contingent world. A bride and groom may pledge themselves together in sincere conviction of their love on their wedding day and then find that their future lives cause their love to diminish. As Bridegroom, God-in-Christ can only offer the promise of his love (as perfect love it will never fail nor diminish) and wait upon the free response of his beloved which may, indeed, change over the years, 'for we share in Christ, if only we hold our first confidence firm to the end' (Heb. 4.14). Even eschatologically, God cannot enforce his will because that would be to deny his identity as Love. In order for the kingdom to be established 'every knee should bow ... and every tongue confess that Jesus Christ is Lord' (Phil. 2.10–11). There is no guarantee that this will ever happen, which is the risk that God takes in creation and redemption and which suggests why so much biblical eschatological language is imaged in terms of a marriage (e.g. Matt. 25.1–13, Matt. 22.1–14). God's love is as vulnerable – and as assured – as human marriage vows. It is always open to rejection or to consummation and partnership. Thus the final triumphant eschatological vision of the Bible is that of a wedding feast (Rev. 21.1–5).

The fullness of God's love, while still awaiting final consummation, has already begun to happen in the life, death and resurrection of Jesus Christ. God has revealed himself in vulnerable honesty, and humans are invited to become his partners by surrendering their lives to him in love. Since self-giving love is what characterizes God, the human believer who freely gives his life to God has already begun to share in the very life of God, to be 'a partaker of the divine nature' (II Peter 1.4).

Sharing in his life means sharing in his will and therefore
contributing to the building up of a responsible human
community of love in which the Old Testament commandments are obeyed not legalistically but in love (Rom. 6.17).
The church is thus spoken of as the Bride of Christ and is the
anticipation of the eschatological community as long as she is
true to her vocation and becomes a community genuine
exchange: mutual respect and delight, encouragement and
overflowing in generous love for one another and (by implication since the kingdom will only be established when every
knee bows and every tongue confesses) for all people.

Surrendering in obedience to the life and will of God will
inevitably open human persons to the rejection which Jesus
experienced, which is why one who truly loves God-in-
Christ must be prepared to 'take up his cross daily' (Luke
9.23). He does this however in the confident hope that,
although living according to the law of love will render him
vulnerable in temporal terms, he is sharing in the life of the
eternal God who can create life *ex nihilo* and thus defeat even
the evil and suffering of the cross.

Thus the Christian believer pledges himself to share in 'his
sufferings, becoming like him in death that if possible I
may attain the resurrection from the dead' (Phil. 3.10–11).
He comes to share in eternal life not as a reward for good
deeds but because in responding to the grace of God with
repentance he comes to unite his own life history with
God's and thus to share in deathless, everlasting life (I John
3.14).

To turn to Christ is to turn towards the life of perfect love,
the sinless life of obedience to God's will which St Paul
images as a marriage ceremony: 'I betrothed you to Christ to
present you as a pure bride to her one husband' (II Cor.
11.2–3).

The coming of the Holy Spirit
R. C. Moberly's insight – that any understanding of the
atonement must include both Calvary and Pentecost – has
already been noted. The scriptural account, though, has two

versions of the Pentecostal experience or bestowal of the Holy Spirit on the disciples: Luke-Acts makes it the particular day of Pentecost (Acts 1) whereas John places it on Easter evening (John 20). It is impossible, and irrelevant, to attempt to coalesce these two accounts, for they derive from the different intentions and cosmological frameworks of the two New Testament writers. However, their insights do complement one another and, if seen as part of the cluster of ideas, stories and images (all of them irreducible to one narrative) which make up the final part of the biblical love story, they can be seen as mutually enriching. That cluster of ideas can be defined together as the importance of human decision and responsibility made in the presence of the absent God.

The self-effacement of the spirit

The presence and absence of God is expressed in the fact that the Ascension and the bestowal of the Holy Spirit are so tightly linked. Matthew and Luke tell of the physical withdrawal of Jesus, and if there is no such specific account in John, the Last Discourses of Jesus serve as a profound commentary on the Synoptic narrative: 'Nevertheless, I tell you the truth: it is to your advantage that I go away, for if I do not go away the Counsellor will not come to you. But if I go I will send him to you' (John 16.7).

The coming of the Holy Spirit brings new gifts to the believers as the epistles all testify. Above all, it brings great responsibility. Once again, it seems that the economy and profundity of John's language is a perfect commentary on the narrative accounts made explicit in Acts and implied in the epistles: in John's account the gift of the Holy Spirit is inextricably linked with the responsibility of sharing in the mission and overflow of God's gracious forgiveness (John 20.22–23).

The Matthean account of that commission makes explicit what the whole story has told: that God has entrusted to his witnesses the responsibility of establishing his kingdom (Matt. 16.19) and in trusting them to do so he has made himself dependent on human response and will. Even eschatologically, God will not enforce his will but will wait upon the free and conscious commitment of his human beloved. Like Jesus, human believers will not be prematurely comforted or rescued by a *deus ex machina* but must become their truly human selves, self-determined to live the joyful and vulnerable life of love, trusting in the continuing presence of the transcendent God and yet living that love *etsi deus non daretur*. This encouraging of humans so to live is the task of the Holy Spirit.

> ... the Holy Spirit effaces Himself, as Person, before the created persons to whom he appropriates grace. In Him the will of God is no longer external to ourselves: it confers grace inwardly, manifesting itself within our very person in so far as our human will remains in accord with the divine will and co-operates with it, acquiring grace, in making it ours.[18]

This self-effacing encouragement of others can define the work of both God the Son, Jesus Christ and God the Father whose intention has always been to encourage the fulfilment of his beloved humanity and to bring her to the point of making a free act of commitment to him. That intention has been made explicit in the life of Jesus, and humans, now living in the Holy Spirit, are made free to become their true selves.

The new responsibility

Any acceptance of a proposal of marriage is an acceptance of new responsibility: each person lives no longer for her self but in and for another. In accepting this marriage proposal, each human person accepts the responsibility of living no longer for herself alone, but in and for God and in and for humans in the corporate community of exchange which is the church and, by anticipation, the kingdom.

Every human marriage involves a voluntary self-limiting of options as the person focusses on his one beloved and keeps faithful to the vows he has made, but in the paradoxical logic of love such limitation brings fulfilment and ever widening horizons. If that is so with human marriage, it is even more so in this covenant, for each believer unites with the immortal and transcendent God, in relationship with whom ever new possibilities emerge.

Indeed, as more and more persons begin to live that life of God's love, then the limitations of the incarnation will be reversed: the man Jesus could only preach in one village at a time but as more and more persons participate and continue his work, the message can be spread in many differing places at once. Obviously, each person will still be subject to the limitations of temporal existence and always limited by the constraints of love (this is why the word 'reversed' is not ideal – the kingdom is only established as long as believers continue the voluntary self-limitation of the incarnation) but in the sharing of the corporate body the limitations will diminish.

The equation of the doctrine of exchange is thus complete. God's self-emptying has filled humanity, his poverty has made many rich.

The Personhood of God

The momentum of this chapter has precipitated the comment at several points that any discussion of God would begin from either the intention of God the Father, the life of Jesus Christ or the activity of the Holy Spirit. Thus the very structure of this chapter has expressed, and compelled us to understand, the process of 'faith seeking understanding' of the early church which was resolved in its formulation of the perichoresis or coinherence of the Trinity.

Creation out of nothing

In a similar way, the examination of this chapter has drawn the conclusion that God's very will is 'to have us live as men without him' and his presence in human lives encourages precisely that. Thus, again, either God or human persons can serve as the non-foundational commencement of this

discussion. One way in which this insight has been traditionally expressed is the doctrine of 'creation out of nothing'
which came to be promulgated in the inter-testamental
period as a reflection upon the story of God's love in the Old
Testament and which, in masterly economy of language,
communicates the paradox of dependence and independence which is the nature of the creature's relationship with
God. It simultaneously expresses

the freedom of the will of God, who did not have to create
the world but chose to do so (i.e. it rejects any idea of the
inevitable emanation of the creation from God);

God's exclusive power to create life;

God's distinctiveness from creation;

the utter dependency of creation on God, because if he
were to withdraw his creative, life-giving love the world
would again fall into chaos;

the independence and integrity of creation;

the goodness of creation which is maintained in existence
by the will of the utterly good God, and which God himself
sees as good.

This formulation (applicable to any of God's creatures but
especially relevant to humanity, whose rational nature
makes possible the dialectical-dialogical encounter of true
love) avoids both the detachment of God discerned in classical theism and the tendency towards pantheism in Process
theology. Indeed, it highlights the fundamental error of
those who argue against Christian belief on the grounds that
it diminishes human value and dignity: the God whose
decline and death were charted in our opening chapter was
never the orthodox, credal Christian understanding of God.
That 'orthodox' God, far from degrading humanity, compels
an appreciation of the freedom, dignity and significance of
human beings.

The economic and immanent Trinity

Even the transcendent God becomes what he is through his
relationship with humanity: their response to him affects and
shapes him into the person he becomes. It is, for example,

conceivable that at any point in the Old Covenant the whole of humanity could have turned to his will, but as they did not he acted to become incarnate and to be crucified, the effects of both of which made him into the person he becomes (as John's account of the wounded hands of the risen Christ and Dante's human face seek to express). Betrayal and rejection have thus made their impression on him both through what others have done to him and how he has responded.

The love of human beings, on the other hand, calls forth his selfhood as together he and his beloved engage in an ever-expanding relationship in which she is constantly amazed and delighted to discover 'the unsearchable riches of Christ' and what she can do and be in relationship with him. This 'becoming' of God is the truth which the traditional idea of the 'economic Trinity' expressed.

The complementary idea of the doxological or immanent Trinity, on the other hand, expressed the self-focussed identity of God 'as he is in himself'. God is Love, from everlasting to everlasting, changeless and perfect. Nothing can alter that. It is this which explains why he is constantly faithful in his love. Both these insights (the economic and the doxological) have to be held in tension. It is one of the deficiencies of classical theism that while it could affirm the impassibility of God it could not include any interaction between God and the world. Process theology, on the other hand, misunderstood the idea of impassibility: interpreting it as non-responsiveness and in doing so failed to affirm the transcendence of God. The dualisms of both schemes meant that neither could conceive of the possibility of eternity 'breaking into' temporal history, the *eschaton* beginning to arrive in the life, death and resurrection of Jesus Christ so that it can be said that there will be no further revelations of him but as Father, Son and Holy Spirit.

What the tensions between these two truths does is to reinforce the statement that the glory of the eternal God is not known in any other way but 'in the face of Jesus Christ'. Once again, the 'scandal of particularity' which has been such an important concept throughout this study is affirmed.

The mutuality of unique persons – the immanent Trinity

The doctrine of the Trinity provides the paradigm, the pattern of the Christian understanding of selfhood: distinct persons sharing in the mutual dependence and independence of relationship in the unity of coinherence or perichoresis.

It is frequently noted that the doctrine of the Trinity expresses that God is Love because the very being of the Godhead is 'communion'. These assertions, however, are not necessarily precisely conceptualized. John D. Zizioulas, on the other hand, makes an intricate analysis in *Being as Communion: Studies in Personhood and the Church* contending that the unity and dynamic of this Trinitarian perichoresis derives its momentum from the person of the Father. This particular insight, deriving from the Greek Fathers (and therefore closely linked with the controversy of 'the filioque clause', which cannot be examined in such a limited space except to suggest that, perhaps, the insights of both the Eastern and Western churches need to be held in a mutually-enriching tension on this subject) maintains that the unity of God and the ontological being of God do not consist in the one substance of God but in the hypostasis of the Father. He is the 'cause' both of the generation of the Son and the procession of the Spirit. As such, his very being is discerned to be freely-willed communion, that is love, not as a secondary attribute or property but as that which is constitutive of his being.

> If God the Father is immortal it is because His unique and unrepeatable identity as Father is distinguished eternally from that of the Son and of the Spirit who call him 'Father'. If the Son is immortal, He owes this primarily not to His substance but to His being the 'only begotten' (note here the concept of uniqueness) and His being the one in whom the Father is 'well pleased'. Likewise, the Spirit is life-giving because He is 'communion' (II Cor. 13.14). The life of God is eternal because it is personal, that is to

say, it is realized as an expression of free communion, as love.[19]

The doctrine of the Trinity, then, is another affirmation that particularity does not destroy relationship but actually enhances it. The 'love' of the Godhead is more precisely defined as the mutuality of unique hypostases or persons freely deriving their identity in relationship with one another.

Face to face with God – the economic Trinity

The paradigmatic quality of the Trinity must not, however, be limited to the immanent Trinity alone as if it were an example set for humans to emulate. The insight of the economic Trinity corrects and enriches this perspective: human selves do not simply mirror the selfhood of the Trinity but are involved in it. The economic Trinity is a conceptualization of the biblical narration of the self-giving of the unique God who shares in a face-to-face relationship of love with human selves, encouraging their self-determined freedom of love.

The persons with whom God is involved and with whom, in love, he not only shares himself but from whom he receives his identity are defined and distinct. Jesus Christ fulfils that perfection of human realization, the one person in history who has been 'truly himself'

> Jesus Christ does not justify the title of Saviour because he brings the world a beautiful revelation, a sublime teaching about the person but because He realises in history *the very reality of the person* and makes it the basis and 'hypostasis' of the person for every man.[20]

Human persons living according to the example of Jesus find their true selves in relation to God and human persons. They then repeat the pattern of relationships in the Trinity: particularity enhanced through mutuality. The full doctrine of the Trinity maintains that this pattern is repeated also in the exchange of selves between God and humans: it is not

Father, Son and Spirit alone who coinhere in the dependence and independence of love but also God and humanity. Both for God as he is in himself (immanent) and as he relates to his creatures (economic) the idea of the Trinity provides the pattern of personhood and, for all the great dissimilarity between God and humans, they are seen to be even more similar.

5

'All That I Am I Give to You':

The Resurrection

Jesus said to her 'Mary'. She turned and said to him in Hebrew 'Rabonni' (which means Teacher). Jesus said to her 'Do not hold me, for I have not yet ascended to the Father and to your Father, to my God and your God.' Mary went and said to the disciples, 'I have seen the Lord' (John 20.16–18).

The resurrection

The resurrection is the focal point of the Christian faith because that faith began with the early Christians' conviction that they had met one who was actually risen from the dead, one whom they had seen crucified. In that experience they believed that they had witnessed the direct action of God, who alone can create life. Here in the resurrection God had acted decisively to break the strict natural law of the finality of death, had acted to explode the categories of understanding by which human beings lived and had revealed his power and freedom to initiate the genuinely 'new thing', to create life rather than simply re-organize existing forms and situations. So to proclaim belief in the resurrection is to proclaim the power of God. However, this power is not of coercion nor of the *deus ex machina* brought in to solve problems. The power of God which has been revealed in the resurrection is but the same power of God which has been revealed before in the suffering of the crucifixion. *It is the power of absolute freedom, which yet trembles with the vulnerability of love.*

Many recent books of theological reflection have focussed on the crucifixion as the supreme revealing of the nature of God as he who shared in the sufferings of his beloved creation, thereby showing that self-sacrificing love is God's very nature. However, as has already been noted in the discussion of Process theology, such an idea has not always been successful in its inclusion of the resurrection.

The attempts to do so have been various but generally unsatisfactory, always faltering in the attempt to integrate the significance of both the crucifixion and the resurrection and to fuse the will of God with his love. The reasons for their failure obviously overlap each other but the following brief survey will, at least, serve to show the features which must be included in any successful presentation: as before, the assertion of God's (and indeed Jesus') freedom to act, his will and loving involvement in history, must be complemented by the distinctive freedom of human decision and activity. Now a similar tension between these two separate events must be introduced which will preserve their separateness as historical events (thereby preserving the tragedy of the crucifixion and the miracle of the resurrection) and yet not destroy the unity of their meaning and significance.

1. The model which places so much emphasis on God's participation in sympathetic suffering with the world has been examined in detail through Process theology and has been found inadequate in its conception of God's activity and freedom. Such passivity does not do justice to God's will nor indeed to his love. Moreover, it does not do justice to the biblical story of Jesus, for his road to the cross was not one of unconscious passivity but willing obedience.

2. The resurrection can be seen as God's sign of approval for what has gone before and for the way in which the full significance of the life and death of Jesus is revealed. It thus reveals Jesus as the supreme agent of God's love and will. This understanding, of which Pannenberg's work *Jesus* –

God and Man is a leading example, is the one which, in many ways, this work follows, but extreme caution must be exercised because it can tend to portray God as a cruel Father who tests his Son's loyalty and then rewards him for having passed the test.

3. On the other hand, the resurrection can be so emphasized as to ignore everything which has gone before as revelatory of God's being. That is the very misunderstanding which such theologians as Moltmann or those of the Process school have tried to counter. It is the 'theology of glory' without the 'theology of the cross', and no more satisfactory today than when Paul chastized the Corinthian church.

4. A variation of this is to see the resurrection as some kind of *deus ex machina*, a miraculous solution to the mistake, disaster or confusion of previous events. The objections to this should be obvious: it sees the events prior to the resurrection as a problem to be solved and thereby hardly revelatory of God's nature. Alternatively, it seems to imply that God was unable to act earlier, thereby implying that his only mode of relationship with the world is that of direct intervention. Finally, if he was able to act but chose not to, that would imply that he was manipulating human beings, giving them the illusion of free-will and self-determination but always intending to override their decisions and activities. Again, it may affirm his will but not his love.

5. Finally, the two events can be seen as non-foundational keys to one another in the longer narrative of the identity of God and Jesus. This approach sees the two events as separate, identifiable events in human history but both revealing the same God. This does not imply an a-historical, mythical dissolution of their significance.

The final understanding of the non-foundationalism of the crucifixion and resurrection relative to each other is the one which will be followed in this chapter, in which discussion of the identity of God (in terms of the nature of his power) and the identity of human disciples (both in this life and after death) will be explored through a focus on the story of the encounter between Jesus and Mary Magdalene (John 20.11–18).

The identity of the risen Christ

The narrative accounts of the resurrection appearances indicate that the historical Jesus and the resurrected Christ must be held together in a mutually enriching tension. The Gospel accounts do assert the correspondence between the two but they also emphasize that they were not exactly co-terminous, for he was not immediately recognizable (e.g. Luke 24.16) and he was not limited by the normal constraints of physical existence (e.g. John 20.19).

As has been previously stated, the language of glorification is more appropriate than suggestions of resuscitation. The sphere of existence which Jesus now inhabits is not of this physical world: the resurrection event and his risen identity cannot be analysed or expressed in solely historical and material terms, for that is to ignore the objective reality of the resurrection and to ignore the nature of time and space in the resurrected presence. Belief in the resurrection 'as it is in itself' demands an openness and wonder at the mystery of the event in which previous categories of human understanding and experience have been transformed.

To use the language of mystery and wonder to suggest that this 'new thing' which God has done has no relation to what has gone before, that it is some kind of *deus ex machina* is not to do justice to the biblical narration, in which the evangelists go to great lengths to establish the real correspondence between the risen Christ and the Jesus whom the disciples knew prior to the crucifixion.

This correspondence militates against viewing the resurrection as a 'timeless' event, only tangentially related to historical space-time. Rather, this correspondence affirms that the resurrection is part of the temporal/historical continuum of the life of Jesus, but the nature of the resurrection event (i.e. its identification with God's initiative to act and create) renders it as the interpretative key for the rest of the continuum. 'The resurrection imposes upon all that has taken place hitherto an entirely different aspect, so that all things began to fall into place and steadily to take on a depth of meaning and consistency impossible to conceive before.'[1]

The appearance of the new creation through the resurrection does not destroy the natural order of space and time: the life histories of the witnesses continue to take place within physical limitations. Yet this history has now been radically re-orientated through the resurrection: the new creation has already impinged upon the old.

Personal identity after death

The subject of death and resurrection is obviously highly complex and it is impossible to enter into a full discussion at this point but it does seem important in a study of human selfhood to give some space to considering the question of the continuity of personal identity after death.

By themselves the resurrection appearances say little about the continuation of life after death because the New Testament witness does not suggest that what happened to Jesus will inevitably happen to others. In other words, the resurrection of Jesus does not affirm the immortality of the human soul. On the contrary, the New Testament consistently states that Jesus did not rise but was raised through the action and initiative of God (e.g. Acts 5.30), and that what has happened to him is also a possibility for others (e.g. Rom. 6.5, I Peter 1.3–5).

The other consistent affirmation is that the death and resurrection was not simply personal to Jesus but of cosmic significance in that sin and evil are destroyed (Rom. 5.6–12) and reconciliation effected between God and humanity (II Cor. 5.14–21).

In order that questions may be asked about its cosmic significance, the resurrection should not be viewed as an isolated incident but rather in the wider context of the life and death of Jesus. There is no need to repeat the detailed arguments of the previous chapter but simply to state that the sinfulness of humanity and consequent estrangement from God has been overcome through the initiative of God who, in the life of Jesus, revealed a perfect human life lived in accordance with the will of God even to the point of death. The life of that one man, who thus shared in the life of God, can only have significance for the world if other people respond to it by recognizing the activity of God in those events. In other words, to extend Moberly's dictum, it is not even Calvary plus Easter which has effected the atonement but these events plus Pentecost.

The question of continuity of human identity after death can, for a Christian, only be answered appropriately in terms of response to Jesus Christ: it is not an abstract question but a christological one to be answered in the context of the biblical narratives of the histories of God and Jesus which coalesce in the resurrection. 'One's destiny is no longer determined by relation to death through sin but through relation to Jesus Christ through faith.'[2] The capacity to recognize God's activity and presence in the life of Jesus (and in a wider context the story of Israel's history and faith) is made, as has been argued earlier, in the power of the Holy Spirit (I Cor. 12.3). The believer receives the promise of the resurrection of his self after death not because of innate immortality but as the fulfilment of God's covenant of love. The believer may hope for eternal life not because of human immortality but because he participates intimately in the life of the transcendent, life-creating God (Rom. 8.9–11).

In the context of this interpretation, two particular points can be drawn from the resurrection narratives. Firstly, they offer the promise of the human person's identity continuing through death so that, as with the selfhood of Jesus, that which a person has become in life is extended through death. The exact form of this selfhood is not known but the narrative suggests that there will be sufficient if not exact continuation.

The physical self

Secondly, the encounter of the two spheres of space-time affirms that even for the Christian believer, physical limitations including death have not actually been destroyed: death, and often pain and suffering, must still be faced by each human being. Indeed, the fact that temporal existence still continues is an affirmation of the unique identity of each person. 'To infinitize the I would mean that the temporal I no longer exists.'[3]

That temporal and physical existence is considered so important to human identity raises one of the most important arguments of this book, which is simultaneously its greatest weakness, as will be acknowledged in the conclusion. The metaphor of human marriage has been deliberately adopted in this work because of its dual emphasis on life-long commitment (as against God as Lover) and physical involvement and self-giving (as against, say, God as Friend or the covenant of a business contract). In sexual love, perhaps more than any other human experience, the self is manifestly physical and not simply an essence *within* a body. This emphasis on the physical is consonant with the doctrines of Creation and Incarnation as well as with the Biblical anthropology of the whole person.

However, in relation to death this raises a problem of understanding: if temporality and physicality are integral to human selfhood how can the continuity of that selfhood be conceived if the specific body of the particular person has been destroyed or is decomposing? This is hardly a new question: St Paul's discussion in the first letter to the Corinthians indicates that it was a problem discerned by the early church, and Thomas Aquinas argued that bodiless souls could not be regarded as human beings.

The issue has been highlighted by Fergus Kerr who has argued in his examination of the theological significance of Wittgenstein that such belief in the incorporeality of the soul is 'that disseminated antipathy to bodiliness which is the last remnant of heretical theology'.[4] He points out that the human refusal to accept creatureliness was, according to biblical testimony, the primordial sin.

His exposition of the philosophy of Wittgenstein is at times reminiscent of various points made elsewhere in this work and at times expands them. The human face, he says, is not just a sign of the distinctiveness of each person nor simply indicative of both the exteriority of the Other and the intimacy of the relationship (as we have argued with reference to the conjunction of 'face to face'). It is also a mark of the sheer physicality of the human being. 'The human body is the best picture of the human soul', says Kerr, and it is particularly in the face that the self is manifest. It is not necessary, or indeed possible, to pass through the body to some deeper essence which is the true self. Gestures, actions and physical expressions are not self-consciously adopted to show feeling and meaning. They are that person's self. Kerr censures Bertrand Russell's dismissal of 'mere' physical habits, contending that the more spontaneous a physical reaction the more genuinely self-related the person may be, and he cites examples which are reminiscent of those used by Polanyi as examples of 'personal knowledge': driving a car or the spontaneous gesture of affection.

Of course, there are occasions of a disjunction between a person's physical actions and his sincerely held convictions. Yet, these are mainly indicative of the diminishment of the self through, for example, lack of freedom or of maturity. Kerr posits the example of believers living in an oppressively enforced atheistic state. An example more appropriate to our theme is a person's failure to enact genuine intention and desire in physical love-making, which would probably be discerned as physical dysfunction or psychological disorder. The same point is made, if arrived at from a totally different angle, in the assertion that sexual crime perpetrated against the body is done against the whole person.

The physicality of the face also expands the idea of 'face to face' encounters: if the self can be discerned in the face then it is true to say that the person who is looking into a face may well discern the selfhood more clearly than the person herself. Kerr, following Wittgenstein, rejects the idea of the individual in a detached 'epistemological solitude' of perfect self-awareness who self-consciously decides to share that self with others. Personal identity is not an individually held possession but is located in the others who see the face and discern the self. In the exchange of selves there is, of course, an experiencing of self-awareness which is part of the mystery of each person. Once again, the example of marriage provides a simple illustration of this paradox. It may be true that after many years of intimacy a wife can know her husband's thoughts and feelings by his face and physical mannerisms. It may be even true that 'she knows him better than he knows himself' in the sense that she can discern, for example, anxiety in his face which he is not yet prepared to admit to himself. However, in a contingent world of distinct persons, she may one day wrongly interpret that same facial expression or physical gesture, in which case he must explain himself from his self-awareness of events and his responses to them in the clarification of verbal communication.

As has already been said, it is because the imagery of marriage can support this affirmation of the physical that it has been chosen for this study, but its very advantage becomes a disadvantage when the question of human death and continuity of identity is raised. There is a similar tension involved in discussing God's involvement with the physical, material world. God's free self-revelation 'in the face of Jesus Christ' does not only refer to 'the scandal of particularity' of Jesus but to the assertion that, as with any person, there is no mysterious essence or 'soul' *behind* the face but the face is the self and reveals the self. There is no God apart from, different to, or even deeper than the one revealed in the physical face of Jesus.

The fact that his face was physical means that in terms of the narrated identification of the self of God, it must be affirmed that God is involved with the physical. In this book, I have attempted to express through the tension of the economic and immanent Trinity and through the use of Jüngel's dictum that 'for all the great dissimilarity between God and humanity, there is still greater similarity'. Again, the imagery of a marriage covenant has offered the possibility of speaking about God's self-giving, which implies physical involvement. Such imagery and language has had to be handled very carefully in order to avoid mythological overtones such as those in the pagan legends of the Sky God consorting with the Earth Goddess, but it has enabled the affirmation and even celebration of the physical demanded by the doctrines of creation and incarnation, and expressed, however inadequately, in the conceptualization of the Trinity.

'The Immortal dies'

When the question of death is brought into the discussion, however, the perspective is changed, for God is seen to be no longer just involved in that which may be celebrated but in the negative, destructive aspect of physicality. In terms of the history of God's identity it becomes necessary to include that which is diminishing. Jüngel argues that it is precisely this 'unity with perishability' with God which is the Christian basis for thinking about God.[5] Accordingly, the phrase 'God is dead' is not adequately interpreted, as we interpreted it in the opening discussion, as a reflection on the demise of classical philosophical theism. Instead, the literal meaning of the motto – that the Immortal dies – must be the true starting point for theological reflection.

Jüngel's choice of the word 'perishability' is significant because it implies negativity and waste and is therefore very different from anything which implies the nobility and dignity of death, and which in the case of Jesus implies a heroic self-sacrifice. The connotations of heroism are perhaps inevitable given the events of the story of Jesus' voluntary self-surrender, but the problem is that such language can underestimate the pain and suffering. It can even give the impression that he did not actually die but was a mythological figure of the dying and rising God whose death was a symbol. The word 'perishability' is more thoroughly and relentlessly negative.

However, Jüngel himself at times appears to be avoiding

the stark reality of death and treating it in a somewhat cavalier fashion as an image or symbol. This is apparent in his discussion about the positive aspect of perishability being 'possibility'. He has a point: the capacity to perish is a sign of life, as simple observation of the natural world confirms. God's involvement in the struggle to bring new life out of that which is perishing confirms that he does respond to suffering. It also confirms his transcendent, life-creating power. However, as I have said, to move too quickly from the rawness of death and suffering is to underestimate them.

Perhaps the events of the life of Jesus partially explain the apparent unwillingness to face up to the diminishment of his self in real death and real perishability. Jesus' death as a young man, terrible and tragic though it was, preserved him from the kinds of suffering endured by so many others, particularly, the process of ageing with its attendant physical and mental deterioration. So much human suffering cannot be conceived of as heroic in any way but only as utterly degrading and wasteful. The development and continuation of human identity in the face of debilitating disease, permanent handicap or dementia is as important an issue as the question of human identity after death. The same irreconcilable paradox is there: the answer of faith wants to say that human identity is not exhausted by physical deterioration, but if the bodily existence is ignored or underestimated it is a subtle dehumanization.

In the non-foundational coinherence which this study is developing, one key element is human death in all the rawness and ambiguity of its finitude. Whatever connotations of heroic self-surrender the crucifixion of Jesus may have it is also true that the face on which Mary Magdalene looked had been brain dead and had stopped breathing. It would, therefore, under the natural laws to which the human Jesus would have been subject, be brain damaged and deteriorated. The body would have been dead for a period of time and would therefore have begun to decompose. It is God's involvement in *that* death, not an image or impression of death, which must be pressed and included in the story of his covenant of love.

The constancy of God's love

Perhaps the only answer is that of Wesley: ''Tis mystery all. The Immortal dies / Who can explore his strange design?', but a too hasty resorting to the idea of mystery does no justice to the capacity of human persons.

> Without a doubt, we must find room in our conceptual scheme for circumscribing the boundaries of that world which we can make intelligible. Yet we must reject the senseless proposal of those theologians who argue that no linguistic proposition is, or ever can be, appropriate with respect to the divine reality. There are many things we do not know and there are many things we know but about which our ancestors had no conception. Nevertheless, this learning process must not be confused with the 'ignorabimus' of the mystery theologian.[6]

In discussing the love relationship between God and humans, the language of mystery is wholly appropriate. However, it must not be used to avoid the rigorous questioning urged by the human intellect, emotions or moral sense, for these are equally appropriate in the honesty of a full human engagement with God.

This tension between wonder and questioning is consistent with the view of humanity as developed in this study, and in relation ö the question of human death and resurrection the image of God as Promiser becomes especially useful and evocative. Until the time of fulfilment, humans must trust God for the future and base that trust on his previous character and on actions experienced in relationship with him. Since humans in love with God are what they are only through that relationship with him, then their identity is grounded in the time and history that they share with God. Personal identity, Helmut Thielicke argues, is not a predication on creaturely nature but is predicated upon the initiative of the life-creating God who addresses humans and upholds them as unique persons before him and with each other. 'The constancy of our identity is the constancy of God's faithfulness.'[7]

The continuity of human history is broken with death, and even after the resurrection of Christ the destructiveness and decisiveness of that death remains. Yet, in Christian trust and hope, our history has become one with God's and we may look forward to life after death.

> To all eternity we are those who are called by name. 'Those with whom God has begun to speak, whether in wrath or in grace, are immortal' (Luther) ... this means that, since the history with God that is the basis of our identity does not cease, we are upheld in our identity even beyond death.[8]

The New Testament witness is, indeed, even more startling than that: the promises have already begun to be fulfilled in the resurrection of Jesus, and the eschatological realm has broken into the realm of physical time and space. Eternity has begun to happen but, again, it can only be understood not as an abstract principle but in christological terms. 'Eternal life is this, to know thee the only true God and Jesus Christ whom thou has sent.'

This new time and history is still 'hid with Christ in God' (Col. 3.3). From outside the perspective of Easter, there is no apparent reality to this life through and beyond death. It is not self-evident but for those who have received the Holy Spirit as a pledge of the promise (cf Eph. 1.13, 14). There is a view beyond death and a new perspective on temporal life itself. They locate their identity in relation to God the Father and this re-orientation of their life can enable them to face death as Jesus did in his earthly life not without dread of the real physical pain (e.g. Mark 14.32–33) but in hope and confidence that, in God, death is no longer the boundary of human existence.

The vulnerability of God's power

The idea that human identity is ultimately upheld by God may seem to imply the denial of human freedom and distinctiveness, to imply that ultimately God overwhelms humans so that there can be no sense of anything approaching equal partnership. This would, indeed, be so were it not for the fact that the resurrection accounts also suggest that God finds his identity in relationship with humans. Both God and humans find their selves in the self-giving re-orientation of their self in the other. The resurrection stories affirm the fullness of God's freedom to act and create life, but that perfect self-relatedness is one of utter selflessness, as I shall proceed to argue.

The crucifixion has often been interpreted in the light of the resurrection and thereby seen as victorious and powerful. The opposite move, in which the resurrection is interpreted in the light of the crucifixion, has been rarely made. Both the crucifixion and the resurrection reveal God's love as vulnerable and fragile, and his power and glory, which they both also reveal, lie in that very fragility.

The problem is that there is an intuitive tendency to see fragility as weakness, and power as something which overcomes that weakness, so that the events of Good Friday and Easter are contorted into an understanding of power and victory in those terms. The alternative approach which is followed here is to approach the story the other way round, allowing our concept of power to be shaped by the events of that story. The very understanding and, indeed, use of the word God depends upon that story, in which his nature is fully and graciously revealed ('All that I am I give to you').

Jesus and Mary Magdalene

The story of the encounter between Jesus and Mary Magdalene by the tomb quivers with vulnerability, the vulnerability of an intimate encounter between a man and a woman sharing their very selves with each other. As Jesus had already voluntarily surrendered himself towards others, becoming dependent upon their response, which was crucifixion, so once again he places himself into another's hands and waits upon her response.

Primarily, this is a story of a face to face encounter in which each partner actually receives her and his identity ('Mary' and 'Teacher'/'Lord') from the recognition and address of the other. 'When Jesus says her name "Mary" with rare intensity and economy John writes for us the moments of recognizing (or remembering) self and recognizing (or remembering God) ... Mary is offered her name, her identity, the name which specifies her as the person with a particular story.'[9]

Her unique story could be thought of as including the repentance and healing of Mary, her loyal discipleship and recent grief as well as the great joy and fulfilment which she found in the love of Jesus. Such a 'selfhood' is based on the various legends of Mary but the concern here is not to define the exact events of her life but to affirm that she was an identifiable, irreplaceable human person.

These experiences and emotions are part of the selfhood which is addressed by the risen Jesus Christ and they will not be obliterated but gathered up and transformed. Her new life involves new responsibility and thus a new identity, being the first person to receive the new commission to proclaim the resurrection. In a sense, however, that new identity will be the person she was before because her proclamation will be made not only through preaching about her belief but mainly through the testimony to, and living out of, her personal story. Ultimately, not her words only but her very self is her most eloquent testimony.

That proclamation will be vulnerable, especially as Mary is a woman whose testimony would not have been considered legally valid. It is not, however, only that which makes the resurrection proclamation vulnerable. Entrusting the message into human hands at all is a great risk, showing that even in the power of his glorification Christ's power is not revealed as coercion or irresistible force but as self-effacing humbleness, and even in the full revelation of his person he still receives his identity from his relationship with human beings. He has now disclosed himself fully to her but still needs her recognition and affirmation of who he is before she will be prepared to spread the message of his divine power.

That recognition will include also an acknowledgment of the new responsibility which is now accepted in her life: living no longer for herself but for God as revealed in Jesus Christ and others in fulfilment of his kingdom. Without human response and co-operation the startling event of the resurrection might well have happened but it could not have had implications for the transformation of human lives and human history.

As in the events leading to the crucifixion, Jesus has voluntarily made himself dependent upon human response, risking the fact that his activity and identity are always open to being ignored or misunderstood and his invitation open to refusal. This is partly the reason why the motif of Jesus as a stranger not immediately or inevitably recognized is so important in the resurrection stories. Mary does not instantly recognize him and she did not have any guarantee that he is 'the Lord' because he stands before her as a human being, indeed one whom she confused with the gardener and who was hardly swathed with the panoply of power and regality normally attributed to the divine.

Thus, even in the resurrection when the power of God (and Jesus Christ) is fully established, that power is shown to be vulnerable because he will not force Mary to respond and cannot guarantee that she will continue to co-operate with him. The words of the risen Christ 'Do not hold me' are not a denial or withholding of his love but quite the reverse. When he pulled away it was not through any fearful refusal to get involved but it was another manifestation of that self-giving and humble love which had marked his relationship with her, because this can be seen as the withdrawal of self which lovers perform for each other, 'making space' so that the other may be free to be herself, not dominated or manipulated by her partner, but actually encouraged and allowed to blossom into her true self so that her self may be shared by them both.

That self-effacing, humble love also characterizes God's relationship with humanity, of whom Mary is but one person. He actively encourages the fulfilment of his beloved's true self by his faithful presence. His presence in her life, as in Jesus', is of the God who is absent and who wills that she become the free, joyful, compassionate and responsible human being who fulfils her mission of exercising forgiving love *etsi deus non daretur*.

In his reflection on the stance of 'face to face', Emmanuel Levinas writes, 'The relation with the Other does not nullify separation. It does not arise within a totality integrating me and the other ... the relation between me and the other commences in the inequality of terms, transcendent to one another ...'[10] In that sense, Jesus looks up to Mary in an attitude of inequality, seeing her as transcendent to him because she can, in the future, do the things he has not done, finish the work of proclaiming the establishment of God's kingdom and 'complete what is lacking in Christ's sufferings' (Col. 1.24).

It is easy to appreciate why Mary should look up to the risen Christ as transcendent to her. The scandal of the Christian faith, however, is that in Jesus God looks up to human beings and sees them as transcendent. As in the understanding of power, so the concept of transcendence ought to be shaped by the Christian story. Thus, as power is there revealed to be vulnerable, so transcendence is there revealed as humility.

The Bride of Christ

Precisely because Mary and Jesus are separate persons they need to communicate with each other, receiving their identity from each other. This addressing and exchange of words will continue in the future when all believers will feel themselves called by name and, convinced that the one who calls them is the Lord, will affirm that conviction by addressing God directly in the language of worship and by sharing their experience with others through the language of testimony. In this compulsion to give verbal

expression to God's love, believers can be seen to be participating in the overflow of God's dialogical being. The
encounter between Jesus and Mary Magdalene prefigures
the future church called into being by the confronting
and inspiring Word of God and which, in turn, responds
decisively to the resurrection by affirming the Lordship of
Jesus Christ.

Although there is no explicit mention of the Holy Spirit
in the passage, this encounter is consistent with the formulation of the effect and activity as made in the previous
chapter: the withdrawal of Jesus from the physical world is
interwoven with both the recognition of the resurrection
and the bestowal of the Holy Spirit. In particular the withdrawal of Jesus encourages her acceptance of such responsibility and it is this which cannot be separated from her
receiving of the Holy Spirit, both willingly and as a gift (cf.
John 16.7).

The mode of God's activity is again as 'the presence
of the absent God', actively encouraging the freedom
and self-determination of Mary. As a free, responsible
and fulfilled person she continues to be sustained by the
promise of eternal faithfulness (Matt. 28.20). As she promises
reciprocal faithfulness, and fulfils that promise in giving
her self away in love, she is drawn into sharing in the
very life of God himself and participating in the divine
nature.

This face-to-face encounter looks forward to the time when
God and human beings will see face to face (I Cor. 13) and
then the knowledge which is now partial, and thus fragile,
will be fulfilled. The paradox is, however, that this partial
knowledge is not a sign of deficiency but of presence: its
fragility lies in the fact that it is the knowledge of love
and therefore, by definition, vulnerable and unenforceable.
Living by faith and in hope is not an inferior knowledge but
the very nature of love. The example of human marriage
vows crystallizes this paradox: the fullness of love exchanged
confidently on the wedding day denies neither its deepening
with the years nor its fragility. This encounter in the garden

and its subsequent deepening are both indicative of God's prevenient presence in the Spirit and anticipate the eschatological 'face to face'.

The scene in the garden may be a particularly important moment in this specific relationship but it cannot be separated from the dynamic of relationships within the wider community of which the two are members, and indeed from the wider activity of God throughout history. Both Jesus and Mary are who they are partly through the influence of and interaction with the many others with whom they have had so many different relationships. That which they have now become must also be shared with others as Mary goes to tell them that Jesus has been raised and to testify to the reorientation of her life.

Precisely because Mary's experience is an anticipation of the future church she might be described as a type of the church, and the metaphor of the church as Bride of Christ may become particularly evocative when seen in the light of her story. Yet the ascription of the Bride of Christ, if it has been identified with any one human figure, has traditionally been given to Mary the mother of Jesus presumably to avoid any implication of the sexuality of Jesus.[11] As has been stated throughout this work, there is no suggestion that a marriage of Jesus and Mary Magdalene is to be given any historical credence. Indeed the fact that they were to be separated plays an important part in their story, so that the vows made by Mary are not made to a historical husband but to God-in-Christ in the eternal covenant of love.

Having said that, however, if Mary Magdalene is spoken of as the Bride it grounds such imagery in reality because they could conceivably have been married, whereas no such possibility is open in the use of the nuptial language about Mary his mother, which must, therefore, be purely symbolic. Mary Magdalene, on the other hand, can be seen not simply as a metaphorical type or figure but as a particular human living in the reality of human history, no more purely an Eve figure than Jesus was an Adam-figure, but a woman working out her Christian discipleship in the contingent problems and opportunities of ordinary human life. Throughout Christian history, the church has been made up of innumerable such brides, male and female, single and married, who have heard the call of God's word and have responded by committing themselves in love.

It would, of course be unwise to contort one particular Bible passage into an overall interpretation but perhaps the very precariousness of such an enterprise is indicative of the language of testimony in which, although there may well be an awareness of problems or other possibilities, nevertheless a person feels compelled to commit himself to one particular understanding of reality. In that spirit I would argue that the dynamic of relationship occurring at the empty tomb bears many resemblances to that of the exchange of vows in a Christian marriage ceremony where one couple takes those intensely personal vows to each other and 'in the sight of God and this congregation'. The exchange is at one and the same time the most intimate thing that they will ever do and a public ceremony. Their relationship is something only that couple can understand and yet one which has been made possible by, and will have implications for the wider community of family and friends of which they are a part. In the same way, this particular moment in time has been made possible by the past and will have implications for the future, bearing a significance out of all proportion to its relative brevity.

Both Mary and Jesus will that their respective histories be no longer separated but that they should share a common history. They thus pledge their whole lives together making themselves dependent upon each other and open to a contingent future, yet open in hope and confidence.

Their separateness-in-unity follows the pattern of the perichoresis of the Trinity but it is more than a mirror image of that unity: because Jesus Christ is the second person of the Trinity and because, through the gracious initiative of the Spirit, Mary participates in the life and mission of God, it follows that the vows which they make to each other

> All that I am I give to you
> All that I have I share with you

are not simply based upon the pattern of the Trinity but may be truly said to be happening 'Within the love of God, Father, Son and Holy Spirit'.

6

Conclusion

In one sense, the structure of this work has exemplified the principle that 'form and meaning' are one: it is, itself, a marriage, a coinherent whole which can only be understood by seeing all parts in relation to one another. It has also exemplified the principle that in non-foundationalism any point may be an appropriate starting-point for a discussion: this work began with a discussion of the complexity of the human person and stated that any adequate modern philosophy, including Christian theology, must include the focus on the human subject which the Enlightenment has precipitated.

That opening section raised the point that the modern decline in religious (and specifically Christian) belief can at least partially be accounted for by the idea that such belief actually degrades human beings. Yet as the work progressed it moved toward the conclusion that the biblical witness narrates that God intends that the value and dignity of human beings should be affirmed and that it is human sinfulness, not God's power, which prevents it from happening. God desires that human beings should live as free, responsible, self-determining persons, an appropriate subject of focus in their own right.

The human experiencing of selfhood is that relationship is a fundamental characteristic of identity: a person feels that he is who he is not in detached isolation but in and through his relationship with others. In this century such a relational understanding has been given a wider context, extending to the insights of quantum physics.

The traditional Christian profession of faith is that such relatedness is grounded in the fact that God is Love and has established the primacy of love in what he has created as well as in the way he himself relates to his creation. If this work was initially encouraged by a conviction that Christian theology must affirm the significance and freedom of human beings, an equally important intuition was from the conviction received from Christian teaching, that God is Love. These two together prompted the criticism that so much traditional teaching of the church has given the impression that God and humanity are set in opposition to one another and that God's power must be emphasized even at the cost of his loving. As was argued at the beginning, this impression is due to the tenets of classical philosophical theism rather than the principles of orthodox biblical Christianity.

The task of this study was thus established as aiming to find a way of speaking about God which emphasized his love and did not degrade human persons. The first approach which was examined was that of Process theology which, with its image of God as Lover, apparently offered the possibility of speaking about the vulnerability of God, his mutuality with humans and even the possibility of God changing. However, it was concluded that this conception of human and divine selfhood was not ultimately satisfactory. God was pictured as incapable of acting freely, and because Process theologians tend to confuse the exercise of power with coercion they thereby maintained the irreconcileable contradiction of God's power and love. It is also unsatisfactory as a commentary on human selfhood because the objectivity and particularity of each person is not emphasized.

It was our definition of love as a re-orientation of one's life in and towards the Other who is objective to oneself which pressed the discussion further and suggested that an answer

lay in the biblical narratives and credal definitions of orthodox Christianity. This was undergirded by the epistemology
of Polanyi and other post-critical philosophers who themselves conceived of knowledge as 'turning to the other' and
participating in the life of that other which yet remains
objective.

One of the most perplexing questions of modern theology
– 'How can the human mind know the transcendent God?' –
was answered by speaking of God's promising. That in itself
was a qualification of the overall picture which was of God as
Husband sharing himself freely in a covenant of love with his
human bride. The contradiction between God's power and
love was resolved, not by denying either of them but by
emphasizing the fragility and precariousness of his love as he
gives responsibility and freedom to his beloved.

Advantages

This picture of a marriage between humans and God, a
partnership of mutual respect and delight overcomes the
objections against classical theism: it avoids the degradation
of human beings into submissive servants which the metaphor
of God as King might countenance and equally avoids the
danger of infantile dependency which might be suggested by
God as Father or Mother. On the other hand, God is
rendered as free and active, not merely reactive, as Process
theology tended towards in its definition.

Individual persons are seen as definable and unique and
therefore of value in their selves and worthy of respect by
others. Yet they are seen within the wider community and
are both shaped by, and shape, that community. The concept
of 'overflow' is particularly important: it implies the interaction between human beings who encounter one another
while yet remaining objective to each other.

Since human beings are rational creatures, their rationality
must be included in any relationship with God. Neither
classical nor Process theism could accommodate the insights
of Einsteinian physics. These systems are, then, not as
intellectually satisfying as the one drawn in this study.

The uniqueness and value of each person, each potentially betrothed to God, means that redemption is not limited to a few. This has important implications for a modern pluralist society which includes those of other faiths and those of no faith who are nevertheless recognized as loving and responsible human beings. This picture affirms the importance, value and dignity of each person, the importance of rejoicing in their distinctiveness, 'giving space' to them and listening to their unique story while at the same time standing by the 'scandal of particularity' which lies at the heart of Christianity and which, Christians believe, actually endorses the value of each person. Similarly, because it speaks of salvation in terms of a process of growing in love, a process ever open to change in a contingent world, there cannot be any sanctioning of an arrogant exclusivism on the part of those who are 'saved'. The Christians' attitude to all others, whatever their confessional stance, must always be humble respect and delight in others, or else they cannot claim to be sharing in the overflow of God's life and love.

Just as human beings are definable and significant, so are individual historical events. History is neither mythologized into 'the flow of history' nor seen as irrelevant. The 'grammar' of time and history is, once again, the principle of co-inherence: definable events are recognized to have happened at a particular point in history and although their significance may extend in time and place, that is not to deny their specificness. So, for example, the crucifixion was a discrete event following a particular train of circumstances and happening 'under Pontius Pilate'. It cannot simply be spoken of as 'self-sacrificing love' nor seen as, say, a type of the sacrifice of Isaac or the death of Abel, for that is to deny its particularity. In this study, as in neither classical nor Process theism, specific historical time is able to bear significance out of all proportion to its chronological length but it nevertheless remains specific historical time.

Finally the modification of this image by the inclusion of the promising of God offers the possibility of speaking about a truly mutual relationship in which all the faculties of the human believer are engaged and yet priority is still accorded to God's initiative. The great advantage of the emphasis on 'promising' is that such language enables belief to be expressed with the certainty of trusting and commitment but without dogmatism and prejudice.

This applies not only to present experience and understanding but can also extend to belief in the future faithfulness of God even after human death. The possibility of being able to use the same image to speak about the present and future accords well with the biblical picture of the *eschaton* having broken into temporal history in the resurrection of Christ.

Disadvantages

God as creator There are disadvantages to the image of God as Husband. For example, it needs to be recognized that the metaphor 'Husband' cannot imply the creative power of either 'Mother' or 'Father'. However, it may equally well be argued that these parental images do not necessarily express mutuality and vulnerability. This reservation simply highlights the point that no one metaphor can adequately express God. In any case, the prevenience and transcendence of God is constantly affirmed in the image of 'Promiser' and the idea of God 'creating out of nothing' is integral to the whole picture.

The gender of God This is a far more serious objection to the picture of 'God as Husband'. As was noted in the discussion of Process theology, the deficiency of applying masculine terminology in relation to God has been well documented in recent years: the quotation from Rosemary Radford Reuther indicates the primary argument that such terminology has sanctioned women's subordination and hierarchical domination models. Perhaps the fifth chapter of the epistle to the Ephesians is the *locus classicus* of interpretation here: Paul argues that the husband has power over the submissively obedient wife just as Christ is autocratic head over his Bride the church.

Yet this study has deliberately chosen to espouse the imagery of 'Husband' in preference to 'Lover', which is neutral in gender. The definition of God as Promiser also avoids gender terms but since it is only a modification of 'Husband' and does not really make sense out of the context of the marriage covenant, it cannot be considered as an adequate alternative.

The impasse thus arrived at is that for strong reasons this work has chosen to use the word 'Husband' to describe God and thereby gives the impression that the masculine must be used to describe perfection and the taking of initiative. The feminine gender is thus used in relationship to dependency, frailty, and imperfection, at best in terms of 'becoming' and at worst in terms of evil. In an attempt to draw a picture of God and humanity which affirms their mutual dignity, have we produced a reactionary image instead?

There might be some value here in remarking that the feminine gender is, in fact, used here and in the Bible to describe human response as a whole: it is Israel or the church which is described as the Bride, not just the women of the community. Some thinkers, perhaps most notably those of the Jungian school of psychology, would see this as symbolizing 'the feminine part' of the human soul (in Jungian terms, the anima) which is especially receptive to the unconscious and religious experience. However, this speculative solution hardly solves the problem because its mythological nature does not take into account either the discrete particularity of persons or historical realism, and gives the impression that there is one part of the human being which is religious, whereas we have consistently argued that the whole person is engaged in a relationship with God. In any case, this idea does not solve the problem of the linguistic equation of feminine terms with imperfect, sinful humanity, and so it does not solve the impasse but merely re-states it.

The answer to the impasse lies in the principles argued throughout the text. God is indeed affirmed to be powerful, prevenient and authoritative, but those terms are defined by his story rather than he being defined by our human understanding. So, as we have argued, power is seen to be vulnerable love, prevenience to be gracious forgiveness, and headship to be humble respect. Feminist theologians are correct in discerning the dangers of traditional terms and in seeking a re-definition of terms. Their mistake is to believe that such a re-definition necessitates a rejection of orthodox biblical and credal Christianity, whereas, in fact, it is orthodox Christianity itself which re-defines our human terms.

For example, what has been written in this book would accord with Dale Spender's re-naming of the language of sexuality. In *Man Made Language*,[1] she suggests that instead of speaking about sexual intercourse as 'penetration' (with its emphasis on the masculine role and its implication of something being done to a passive female by an active male) the word 'enclosure' might be used. The implications of this word are quite different and quite in accordance with the principles of self-giving, voluntary dependency and participating in the life of another who is honoured and obeyed.

If such terminology can be applied to wider systems, classical theism posited God penetrating the world whereas in Process theism the partner's discreteness was so obscured that it is difficult to envisage any encounter. The orthodox Christian picture, on the other hand, shows God allowing himself to be enclosed in his beloved, accommodating himself to her experience and giving himself freely and joyfully, yet still retaining his separate identity. The problem encountered in reading Ephesians chapter five, I would suggest, is that the profoundly radical understanding and re-definition of 'headship' and 'authority' initiated by the Christian story have yet to be rigorously applied.

'Feminist theology' covers a vast range of writers, ideas and insights and it is unfair to assess such a range in this short space. Nevertheless, it must be said that the fundamental mistake of feminist theologians is that they have not engaged fully with the Christian story, understood why it developed and allowed their understanding to be shaped within it. For example, the Old Testament emphasis on the transcendence of God was not primarily intended to affirm male superiority but rather to emphasize the power of the Creator who could create the genuinely new, as opposed to the animistic deities of the Goddess religion whose creativity was bound within the cycle of seasons. Similarly, the doctrine of the Trinity was not formulated as a piece of arbitrary speculation but in response to God's revelation of himself in history. As such the designation of Father, Son and Holy Spirit is irreplaceable and cannot be substituted by, say, 'Creator, Redeemer and Sanctifier'[2] and certainly not by a 'feminine Trinity of the three Marys at the tomb'[3], as if the saving efficacy lay in the number three rather than in the story of God's love.

This is not to say that there has not been masculine domination and oppression nor to deny the presence and value of feminine imagery of God nor to ignore the attitude of Jesus towards women. However, it is to assert that the 'scandal of particularity' at the heart of the Christian faith makes the predominance of masculine language in relation to the Godhead inevitable: for this is the story of a particular historical man and his relationship with God, whom in his cultural tradition he called 'Father'. To empty that story of its particularity is ultimately to deny the uniqueness of each person.

Rosemary Radford Reuther is correct when she writes that it is 'of no ultimate significance' that Jesus was male.[4] However, she is not right in the sense that she intended – an ignoring of his maleness so that he might be called 'Christ in the form of our sister' – for that is to posit a mythological androgyne rather than a historical person. It is incidental that Jesus was a man in the sense that in a contingent world it is possible that the Saviour could have been a woman but the 'scandal' of his particularity (including his 'maleness') affirms the scandal of particularity of all persons (whether male or female) as their own irreplaceable, infinitely valuable self.

Feminist theology, like Process theology, tends to confuse objectivity with detachment, and the taking of initiative with coercion. Their answer to the domination models and sanctioning of oppression is to create an egalitarian model of God's relationship with humanity.

Yet the question must be asked, 'Where is the reason to hope in such a God?' In the face of human degradation and oppression, hope cannot lie solely or even primarily in the humanity whose sinfulness has made such oppression but in the God who can take the initiative to restore right relationships, who has the transcendent power to bring life 'out of nothing' and in relationship with whom human beings become the responsible, caring persons who build up a community of true exchange. This is the biblical and credal picture, compared to the thrilling dynamism and hopefulness of which Process and feminist theology seem sadly prosaic and static.

'Till death us do part' Human marriage vows pledge the couple to faithfulness in the face of the 'for better, for worse' events of a contingent world. There is, however, one event which may end that faithfulness – the death of one of the partners. The covenant is then nullified and the other is free to choose another partner.

Any one metaphor of, or language about God, is inadequate to express the mystery of God's being and the depth of his love. This picture of the marriage partnership between God and humanity is evocative and useful in many ways. However, in this very picture lies its own criticism which militates against any complacent conclusion that we have arrived at a perfectly systematic definition of divine and human selfhood: for God's selfhood and his faithfulness is not nullified or exhausted by physical death and there is thus apparently no way in which God and his bride can meaningfully say 'Till death us do part'.

Postscript

As this study developed the exchange of marriage vows, rather than the married state became the controlling metaphor. In conclusion, therefore, the focus will be on the picture conveyed by these words:

All that I am I give to you
All that I have I share with you
Within the love of God, Father, Son and Holy Spirit.

This picture of bride and groom standing face to face does suggest their distinctiveness combined with their union. It also implies commitment to one particular person and that element of 'once-for-all' is intensified since one specific time and place are intended to bear such great significance for the whole of their lives.

As they turn to face each other, there is full awareness of their intention and complete freedom to will that intention into action, but that freedom is actually enhanced by a sense of compulsion to surrender their selves in vulnerable dependency upon each other, and that will is not only active now but is pledged to remain constant in the face of the very real contingencies of the future. The physical action of the ceremony and the linguistic address of the words are indicative of the person's intention and in that sense are the person's presence but ultimately each partner trusts not in the action nor in the words but in the integrity and fidelity of the other. The words 'all that I have' ground the promises firmly in material reality. Finally, the words 'Within the love of God, Father, Son and Holy Spirit' point towards God who, in his Trinitarian identity, provides a mirror of the identity of the couple but who goes further than that and even invites humanity to participate 'within' his divinity.

George Macdonald once described God as the one who is eternally self-abandoning. 'If there were such a thing as self always giving itself away, that self would be God.'[1]

The continual self-giving, kenosis, characterizes Father, Son and Holy Spirit. It is this kenosis which allows the possibility of a relationship in which both God and human believers are able to say as a bride and groom might well say at the exchange of their vows:

> And for me it is a necessity of love
> this gift of myself,
> this placing of myself in your hands
> without reserve
> and in boundless confidence
> because you are my Love.[2]

NOTES

1. *Introduction: Divine and Human Selfhood*

1. In order to avoid the excessive use of the masculine pronoun which might sound sexist, and yet also needing to avoid the clumsiness of continually writing 'he' or 'she' I have decided to use the words 'he' 'she' interchangeably as the personal pronoun throughout this book.

2. Jürgen Moltmann, *The Crucified God*, SCM Press 1974, p. 249.

3. Jürgen Moltmann, *The Experiment Hope*, SCM Press 1975, p. 73.

4. Thomas Aquinas, *Summa Theologiae*, 1a, q. 13, art. 7.

5. John Macquarrie, *Thinking About God*, SCM Press 1975, p. 111.

6. Schubert Ogden, 'Love unbounded: The Doctrine of God', *The Perkins School of Theology Journal*, 19, 3 (Spring 1966), p. 16.

7. Walter Kasper, *Jesus the Christ*, Burns and Oates 1976, p. 82.

8. Norman Pittenger, *Picturing God*, SCM Press 1982, p. 77.

9. Eberhard Jüngel, *God as the Mystery of the World*, T. & T. Clark 1983, p. 320.

10. John Macquarrie, *The Humility of God*, SCM Press 1978, p. 66.

11. Jüngel, op. cit., pp. 343–368.

2. *God as Lover: Process Theology*

1. Norman Pittenger, *Picturing God*, SCM Press 1982, p. 100.

2. Alfred North Whitehead, *Process and Reality*, The Free Press, New York 1929, p. 141.

3. Charles Hartshorne, *The Divine Relativity*, Yale University Press 1948, p. 8.

4. Colin Gunton, *Being and Becoming: The Doctrine of God in Charles Hartshorne and Karl Barth*, OUP 1978, p. 21.

5. John Cobb and David Griffin, *Process Theology: An Introductory Exposition*, Belfast 1976, p. 28.

6. Alfred North Whitehead, *Process and Reality*, p. 50.

7. Norman Pittenger, *Process Thought and the Christian Faith*, SCM Press 1968, p. 40.

8. Cobb and Griffin, op. cit., p. 61.

9. Rosemary Radford Ruether, *New Woman: New Earth*, Crossroad Publishing Co., New York 1975, pp. 74–75.

10. St John of the Cross, *The Dark Night of the Soul*.

11. Norman Pittenger, 'Trinity and Process', *Theological Studies*, 322, June 1971, p. 296.

12. Cobb and Griffin, op. cit., p. 53.

13. Ibid., p. 132.

14. 'More Songs from Vagabondonia', quoted by Norman Pittenger in *The Lure of Divine Love*, Pilgrim Press, New York 1979, p. 73.

15. Colin Gunton, op. cit., p. 220.

16. Ibid., p. 221.

17. Ibid., p. 41.

18. See Marina Warner, *Alone of All Her Sex: The Myth and Cult of the Virgin Mary*, Quartet Books 1978, pp. 224–235; Robert Murray, *Symbols of Church and Kingdom*, CUP 1975, pp. 332–333; Elisabeth Moltmann-Wendel, *The Women Around Jesus*, SCM Press 1982, pp. 61–90. For a fictional account of such an idea see Michele Roberts, *The Wild Girl*, The Women's Press 1984.

19. Both 'Love-in-Act' and 'Loving Activity in the World' are terms used by Pittenger in *Picturing God*. The term 'God as Verb' is used by Mary Daly in *Beyond God the Father*, The Women's Press 1973, which should strictly be classified not as Process theology but radical feminism. However, as there is an interweaving of these two schools of theology, the point is still valid.

20. Cobb and Griffin, op. cit., p. 98.

21. Thomas Torrance, *Divine and Contingent Order*, OUP 1981, p. 54.

22. Daniel Hardy, 'Christian Affirmation and the Structure of Personal Life', in Torrance, *Belief in Science and Christian Life*, The Handsel Press 1980, p. 87.

3.   *Knowing and Loving: Questions of Knowledge*

1. A. R. Peacocke, *Creation and the World of Science*, OUP 1979, p. 56.

2. Hans Georg Gadamer, *Truth and Method*, Sheed and Ward 1975.

3. Michael Polanyi, *Personal Knowledge*, Routledge 1958, p. 300.

4. Ibid., p. 312.

5. Ibid., p. 309.

6. Andrew Louth, *Discerning the Mystery: An Essay on the Nature of Theology*, OUP 1983, p. 56.

7. Polanyi, *Knowing and Being*, Routledge 1969, p. 138.

8. Thomas Torrance, *The Mediation of Christ*, Paternoster Press 1983, p. 17.

9. Thomas Torrance, *Theological Science*, OUP 1969, p. 132.

10. Ronald Thiemann, *Revelation and Theology: The Gospel as Narrated Promise*, Notre Dame University Press 1985.

11. Torrance, *Theological Science*, pp. 97–98.

12. Ibid., p. 299.

13. Thiemann, op. cit., p. 43.

14. Ibid., p. 75.

15. Ibid., p. 109.

16. Ibid., p. 110.

4. 'I Will Be Your God . . .': The Bible as Love Story

1. Hans Frei, *The Identity of Jesus Christ*, Fortress Press, Philadelphia 1975.

2. Karl Barth, *Church Dogmatics*, vol. III, part 1, T. & T. Clark 1961, p. 313.

3. Alan D. Galloway, 'Creation and Covenant' in Richard McKinney (ed), *Creation, Christ and Culture*, T. & T. Clark 1976, p. 112.

4. From an unpublished paper by Nicholas Peter Harvey, *Thinking Theologically About Death*.

5. Dietrich Bonhoeffer, *Letters and Papers From Prison*, The Enlarged Edition, SCM Press 1971, p. 360.

6. Rosemary Haughton, *The Passionate God*, Darton, Longman and Todd 1981, pp. 177ff.

7. See John Hick (ed), *The Myth of God Incarnate*, SCM Press 1977; S. W. Sykes and J. P. Clayton (ed), *Christ, Faith and History*, CUP 1972; Michael Goulder (ed), *Incarnation and Myth: The Debate Continued*, SCM Press 1979.

8. For the detailed argument of this point see Thiemann, op. cit., pp. 112–140. For the argument about the narration of King David's election see Thiemann, pp. 88–89.

9. John Milbank, 'The Second Difference', *Modern Theology*, 2, No. 3, April 1986, p. 222.

10. Colin Gunton, *Yesterday and Today*, Darton, Longman and Todd 1983, p. 101.

11. Elizabeth Ruth Obard, *Magnificat*, Darton, Longman and Todd 1985, p. 75.

12. See, for example, Vladimir Lossky, *In the Image and Likeness*, Mowbray 1975.

13. Translation by Dorothy L. Sayers, Penguin 1962, p. 346.

14. Guerric of Igny, *Liturgical Sermons*, Cistercian Publications 1971, p. 173.

15. John A. T. Robinson, *The Human Face of God*, SCM Press 1973, p. 64.

16. Donald MacKinnon, 'The Relation of the Doctrines of the Incarnation and the Trinity' in Richard McKinney, op. cit., p. 104.

17. R. C. Moberley, *Atonement and Personality*, London 1909.

18. Vladimir Lossky, *The Mystical Theology of the Eastern Church*, James Clarke 1957, pp. 172–73.

19. John D. Zizioulas, *Being as Communion: Studies in Personhood and the Church*, Darton, Longman and Todd 1985, p. 48.

20. Ibid., p. 54.

5. 'All That I Am I Give to You': The Resurrection

1. Torrance, *Space, Time and Resurrection*, OUP 1969, p. 164.

2. Ray S. Anderson, *Theology, Death and Dying*, Blackwell 1987, p. 75.

3. Ibid., p. 111.

4. Fergus Kerr, *Theology after Wittgenstein*, Blackwell 1986, p. 140.

5. Jüngel, *God as the Mystery of the World*, T. & T. Clark 1983, pp. 184–225.

6. Steven T. Katz, 'The Language and Logic of "Mystery" in Christology' in S. W. Sykes and J. P. Clayton (eds), *Christ, Faith and History*, CUP 1972, p. 254.

7. Helmut Thielicke, *Being Human . . . Becoming Human*, Doubleday, New York 1984, p. 89.

8. Ibid., p. 91.

9. Rowan Williams, *Resurrection*, Darton, Longman and Todd 1987, p. 44.

10. Emmanuel Levinas, *Totality and Infinity*, Duquesne 1969, p. 196.

11. See Marina Warner, op. cit., pp. 121–176.

6. Conclusion

1. Dale Spender, *Man Made Language*, Routledge 1980.

2. Sara Maitland, *A Map of the New Country: Women and Christianity*, Routledge 1983, p. 174.

3. Elisabeth Moltmann-Wendel, *A Land Flowing with Milk and Honey*, SCM Press 1986, pp. 188–191.

4. Rosemary Radford Reuther, *Sexism and God Talk*, SCM Press 1983, p. 137.

Notes # Notes 151

Postscript

1. George MacDonald, *Wilfrid Cumbermede*, Kegan Paul, London, (n d), p. 308.

2. Charles de Foucauld, 1858–1916. This prayer of dedication is taken from Carlo Carretto, *In Search of the Beyond*, Darton, Longman and Todd 1975. The original last word was 'Father' but I have changed it to 'Love' as appropriate to this work. Used by permission.